Which? Way to Manage Your
Time – and Your Life

About the author

A pharmacologist by training, Mark Greener is now a medical journalist and editor, who has contributed to both consumer and specialist publications, including *Health Which?*. He has written widely on the subjects of drugs, nutrition, health and the pharmaceutical industry for medical, nursing and consumer magazines, and is the health editor for *Pharmaceutical Times*. For Which? Books he has written *The Which? Guide to Managing Strees* and *The Which? Guide to Managing Asthma*.

Which? Way to Manage Your Time – and Your Life

Mark Greener

 CONSUMERS' ASSOCIATION

Which? Books are commissioned and researched by
Consumers' Association and published by
Which? Ltd, 2 Marylebone Road, London NW1 4DF
Email address: books@which.net

Distributed by The Penguin Group:
Penguin Books Ltd, 27 Wrights Lane, London W8 5TZ

First edition September 2000

British Library Cataloguing-in-Publication Data
A catalogue record for this book is available from the British Library

ISBN 0 85202 835 0

For a full list of Which? books, please write to Which? Books, Castlemead,
Gascoyne Way, Hertford X, SG14 1LH, or access our web site at www.which.net

The author and publishers would like to thank the following for their comments on the text:
Liz Jones, Sue Davies, Sue Freeman, Emma Copeland, Roger Moore (Consumers' Associaiton);
Lindsey Etchell and Andrew Day (Ricability); Virginia Wallis

Cover and text design by Kysen Creative Consultants
Cover photography designed by Sarah Watson

Typeset by CentraServe Ltd, Saffron Walden, Essex
Printed and bound in England by Clays Ltd, Bungay, Suffolk

Contents

★An asterisk next to the name of an organisation in the text indicates that the address can be found in this section

Introduction

Perhaps it is not surprising that so many of us feel dissatisfied with our lives. Research has revealed marked disillusionment among many ostensibly successful people, reflecting a feeling that our lives today are out of balance. Despite modern technology and labour-saving devices, we now seem to work harder than previous generations. A recent survey on 'the quality of work life' found that 10 per cent of managers in Britain work more than 61 hours a week. The British now work the longest hours in Europe. In contrast, some French companies are moving towards a four-day week.

These long working hours are made even longer by commuting, and working late has become a leading cause of tension in marriages. Organisations are facing a growing number of lawsuits as employees seek compensation for work-related stress. The north-west region of the Engineering Employers Federation, for example, reported a three-fold increase in claims for stress-related illness over six months, according to a report in the *Financial Times* in April 2000. Recent settlements have been at the level of about £200,000.

Even if things do not go this far, rising levels of stress coupled with poor time and life management can reduce productivity, leave people tired and even contribute to some diseases. The Health & Safety Executive estimates that one in five employees takes time off because of work-related stress. Indeed, stress-related illnesses account for 60 per cent of absenteeism. The total cost to industry could reach £6.4 billion a year.

On the other hand, as this book shows, controlling your time – and your life in general – reduces stress, boosts productivity and helps you get more out of life at work and at home. Indeed, the advice, suggestions and strategies in the book should help you find ways

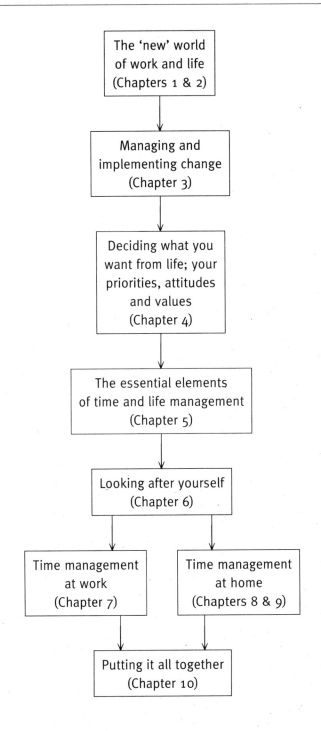

around some fundamental problems at work, such as the so-called 'glass ceiling', job insecurity and flatter corporate structures.

Almost 40 years on from the rise of women's liberation, women at work still face considerable and persistent problems. For example, the government's report *Social Inequalities*, published in May 2000, found that women working full time earn 30 per cent less than men. This applies in both traditionally female jobs, such as hairdressing, and more male-dominated fields, such as engineering and the law. Ironically, the need to overcome these problems has led women to develop life strategies that may be more appropriate for dealing with our changing world than those traditionally employed by men.

This book offers some suggestions to help people rise to the challenges thrown up by a world in which change appears to be the only constant. Certainly, few of our grandparents would recognise the sorts of working lives most people have today. Twenty years ago, only 40 per cent of families had mothers and fathers who worked outside the home. Today, that figure is 60 per cent.

Moreover, technology is moving forward at an ever-increasing pace. How many of us had used – or even heard of – the Internet ten years ago? How many of us had mobile phones? Today both are commonplace and in early 2000, according to a Netprofit survey, 43 per cent of us owned mobile phones, 37 per cent of homes contained personal computers and 27 per cent of homes had Internet access. All these figures will rise.

Such technological advances can make life easier. However, we may sometimes feel we are in danger of being burnt by the white heat of technology. The speed of email and electronic communication puts us under pressure to work, and hence to live, at an ever more hectic pace. Moreover, mobile phones and laptop computers make it more difficult to leave work behind as we close the office door. So this book will look at ways in which we can tame modern technology, rather than becoming a slave to it. For some of us that may mean ignoring the hype and *not* having a mobile phone, palmtop or other computer.

Many of the old certainties, such as that a job, or marriage, is for life, are gone. We also face a proliferation of choice – but often in trivial, peripheral areas, such as the choice offered by digital television. Such proliferation takes time and demands our concentration as we exercise the choice – hence, more pressure.

More fundamentally, these time thieves at home, at work and in society can distract us from what really matters. Yet we want, perhaps to a greater extent than our parents, to make the most of our lives and to live out our dreams, hopes and aspirations. The tension between the lack of time and our aspirations threatens to throw us off balance and can cause considerable stress. Even our families suffer. The National Work Life Forum reported in May 2000 that half of all fathers now spend less than five minutes with their children each day: what proportion of those fathers truly believe that this is enough?

Clearly, we all need to strike a balance between time spent at home and time spent at work. Indeed, leading management consultants now recognise that helping employees restore such a balance improves productivity. One American oil tycoon went so far as to fire people who worked late. In Britain, large corporations are adopting specific policies to lower excessive working hours. You can draw on some of these strategies and apply them to your life.

Surviving and thriving in a changing world means looking beyond conventional time and life management and career planning. It means making informed – sometimes difficult – choices about how we spend our time, some of which would have been an anathema a generation ago. For instance, a 1998 survey of BT's senior managers found that 38 per cent of staff refused promotion because of the detrimental effect on their life outside work. Yet according to another survey, UK@Work 2000, funded by a workplace consultancy, 60 per cent of workers felt that their employers failed to recognise their need to balance life in the office and at home.

This book deals with the issues raised above and how they affect life both at work and at home. The flow diagram on page 8 shows its structure, so that if you wish you can dip in and out to see how you might tackle specific problems rather than reading the book through from start to finish. It will spend almost as much time helping you decide what you are going to build and how to draw up plans. Regardless of your aims in life, the ideas, techniques and strategies outlined in the pages that follow should help you reach your goals more easily.

Chapter 1

From the log cabin to the board room

The fact that you are now reading this book suggests that you probably feel that there is insufficient time to do everything you need or want to do at home and at work. Perhaps you would like to spend more time with your family, or have the opportunity to indulge in your hobbies more fully. Or perhaps you simply feel weighed down by the demands of work. If this sounds all too familiar, take some consolation in the fact that you are not alone. A survey by Abbey National (1991) found that 70 per cent of those polled reported problems managing their time. And in a survey of US readers (May 2000), *Good Housekeeping* found that two-thirds of its respondents claimed they were too tired for sex.

Today, almost everyone, in every stratum of society, thinks that they are under increasing pressure. Yet tragically, many of us waste time, our most precious resource, by performing habitual, inefficient activities that bring us little satisfaction and a great deal of stress. To compound the problem, ever more demands are placed on our time. We are beset by the requirements of longer and longer working hours, and, for those with children, the need to nurture our offspring through education and play make it hard to find any time of our own. So when do we have the opportunity to explore our own interests, talents and opportunities? Perhaps this is why so many of us share the feeling that 'there must be more to life than this'.

Everyone has responsibilities that they cannot avoid. Everyone needs to earn a living or look after a home. Everyone has hopes, dreams and ambitions. And everyone faces the same dilemma: with just 168 hours in a week, how do you decide how to spend that time? Because we all share this same fundamental problem, time and life management is not just for yuppies. It is for everyone who wants to gain greater control over his or her life.

If there were an infinite amount of time, balancing our conflicting demands would not be a problem, of course. However, in the real world most of us find that our lives are out of balance at some time or another. For some, life may even be teetering on the brink of chaos. Trying to cram our commitments to employers, families and ourselves into a limited time causes stress, and stress exacerbates numerous ailments from heart disease, to cancer, or mental illness. Not surprisingly, the link between stress and time pressure catches you in a spiral: you are stressed, so your performance suffers, and that means you cannot do as much in your limited time; you become more stressed, and so your performance declines further.

Imposing order on chaos

Fortunately, there are ways in which you can impose some order on this chaos and make the most of your limited time. The key to life management is, ironically, to look beyond time management. There are numerous tricks and techniques (many of which you will find within these pages) that can maximise your productivity. But this book aims to go beyond such devices to explore the ways by which you can balance the demands on your time and progress towards your life goals. The book offers ways to help you define what these goals really are and discover what may be holding you back when you strive for them. After all, reaching your goals is really the point of effective time and life management. Otherwise, performing more effectively may amount only to travelling faster on a road to nowhere.

Many hard-nosed managers and executives may worry that this sounds a bit soft. However, leading management consultants to many of the world's largest corporations now recognise that helping employees restore a sense of balance in their lives improves productivity. Moreover, those consultants counselling managers and executives now suggest that to survive and thrive in a world in which the only certainly is uncertainty means looking beyond conventional job descriptions and career plans. It also means looking beyond conventional time and life management techniques. To thrive necessitates developing time management into 'life management'.

In essence, the hundreds of tips that you can use to free your time at home and at work aim to make your life simpler. However, living simply does not necessarily mean living in the austerity of a log cabin. Rather, it means organising your life so that you do not waste your time on pointless activities that do not take you any closer to what you want out of life. The management techniques outlined in this book are tools that allow you to simplify and get the most from your time and life.

Beyond time and life management

'Too much time and life management,' notes the management guru Brian Clegg in a recent article in *Professional Manager*, 'is focused on time. Although it does come into it, it's only a secondary factor because real time and life management has to be about your personal priorities.' Against this background, Clegg suggests deciding which time and life management principles, ideas and resources work for you. From your choices you can build a time and life management tool kit to call on as and when you need it. Throughout this book you will find the principles, ideas and resources that allow you to develop your own personal tool kit.

John Adair, another business consultant, makes a related point in his book *Time Management and Personal Development*. He argues that we should regard time as our 'most precious commodity – to be spent carefully and generously'. This attitude, he suggests, should be an essential element in one's philosophy of life. Indeed, if you control your time, you control your life, and this is the idea that broadly underlies the concept of 'life management'.

You do not have to undergo a Jekyll and Hyde personality change to gain control over your life. Accumulating small changes in your behaviour allows you to transform your life. However, changing your behaviour in one area probably will not be enough. What is needed is a comprehensive approach that allows you to manage your work, personal and family life.

The accelerating pace of life

Whether or not our lives are more stressful today than in, for example, the Stone Age or the Victorian era is an open question. The threats may have changed – from, say, a sabre-toothed tiger to working in a pit or factory, or to the present-day fear of unemployment. However, one thing is certain: the quickening pace of life means that we need to manage our time more effectively than did our ancestors. Until the mid-nineteenth century, the sun governed life and most people needed to cram most things they had to do into the daylight hours. Only those who could afford candles avoided traditional work patterns based on night and day.

Indeed, sundials were the most accurate way of keeping time until, as recently as the mid-nineteenth century, when the Greenwich Observatory began sending time signals by telegraph. Until then, even clocks and watches were set by the local sundial, and, in this way, towns decided their time individually. It was the spread of the railway network that eventually standardised time and Greenwich Mean Time became the legal standard in 1880.

Today, the world is changing faster than ever. We can stay busy 24 hours a day thanks to the electric light bulb and, as a result, the standard nine-to-five work day is rapidly becoming an anachronism for many people. About one million people in the UK are still at work between 9 p.m. and 11 p.m. and 300,000 work between 2 a.m. and 5 a.m. These figures may double over the next few years. (Most of the new army of nocturnal workers are women.)

At the same time, society is changing because of an explosion in consumer choice. On first reflection, this may seem to be a good thing: after all, variety is the spice of life. But all too often the choices are in trivial or peripheral areas of life. Rather than making life richer, the proliferation of, often rather mundane, choice simply steps up the pressure. What we are left with is just an ever-increasing number of ways to keep up with the Joneses. We can now choose between hundreds of digital television channels, but how many will we really watch? We can choose between millions of web sites, but how many are useful to us? Dental floss is another case in point. In the 1970s, consumers in Britain could choose from 12 types of dental floss, *Newsnight* (BBC Television) reported in 1999. Now there are more than 64 and just choosing between them takes time.

So much of the faster pace of life seems ultimately pointless. Do we really need to get our holiday photos developed the same day? Are we so pushed for time that we need to buy our fast food even faster by using 'drive-through'? Is the time gained by speeding really worth the risk of an accident? Yet, these trends conspire to produce a feeling that we *need* and *have* to live at a hectic pace, or else risk missing out on something (though exactly what is never clear). As a result, many people feel that they cannot find the time for the things that really matter to them.

Even professionals, who one might expect to be more content with their lot than most, are becoming more and more disillusioned. This was underlined a couple of months into the new millennium when Voluntary Service Overseas (VSO)★ reported a dramatic rise in applications from professional adults, and especially from those with business and managerial backgrounds.

Part of the reason for the disillusionment seems to lie in a growing 'post-consumerist blues'. Independent research commissioned by VSO suggests that, despite their status and relative affluence, many professionals remain dissatisfied. The survey laid the blame on our 'stress-and-spend' lifestyles (an issue discussed in Chapter 2). For example, an opinion poll commissioned by VSO found that among the general public:

- 94 per cent believe that Britain is becoming more materialistic
- 84 per cent agree that British people are under too much pressure to spend
- 89 per cent believe that people in Britain increasingly expect to have it all
- 84 per cent think this 'have it all' attitude is ruining our children's lives
- 81 per cent say that however much they earn, it never seems enough
- 64 per cent wish they could lead a simpler life
- 32 per cent say they need more time and space to themselves above all else.

The survey highlights a widespread, fundamental unhappiness with society's current values, even among those people who have done well in their professional lives. In part, this disillusionment may reflect the fact that many of society's old certainties − such as that a professional job is for life − have disappeared.

More hectic lifestyles, changed working patterns and the break-down of traditional gender roles mean that some of life's little rituals, the landmarks in the day, are slowly being eroded as well. For example, twenty years ago we spent an hour a day cooking and half an hour eating the family dinner. Now that is down to 20 minutes cooking and 10 minutes eating. While cooking can be a chore, at least longer mealtimes offered an opportunity to talk to your children and spouse.

The rise of home working

Another recent trend that is fundamentally changing society is the dramatic rise in the number of people working from home. Around two million people in the UK already work from home and the number is growing. BT estimates that one in four people will work from home by 2025. Increasingly, companies encourage telecommuting, whereby employees use computer terminals away from the office, either at home or at one of the newly emerging telecentres (see below). It certainly makes economic sense. Some companies are able to reduce office space by up to 70 per cent, which can mean large savings on their overheads, and increase productivity by similar amounts. In theory, this working practice should allow employees to manage time better and keep their lives balanced. However, being in charge of your working life means managing your time more effectively, and that requires greater discipline.

Teleworkers, telecentres and telecottages

The rise of home working is directly related to the increased power of the personal computer, which enables many former office workers to carry out tasks from home using computer terminals with links to main offices. Meeting the needs of these 'teleworkers' is a growth industry. For example, telecentres offer local office space for teleworkers who prefer not to work from home because of the isolation, lack of space or to make use of the facilities that a centre may provide. Another newcomer is the telecottage, which provides a resource for local communities to develop the skills needed in the new, multimedia world.

As can be seen, time and life management is about more than choosing between a personal organiser and a palmtop computer. It is about finding the time to discover what matters to you and planning how to get it. It is about visualising the big picture, and finding the time for continual learning and development. And it is also about looking after your physical and mental health. Only this kind of holistic approach will allow you to survive and thrive in a world where change is the only certainty.

Ten strategies for surviving and thriving in a changing world

Management consultants believe that certain principles offer a framework for survival in the changing world. You can hang the time and life management techniques discussed later in the book on to this framework. For example, Trix Webber, a management researcher at Brighton University, proposed (in *Career Development International*) ten 'survive and thrive' strategies from a business perspective. Because these strategies fundamentally rely on efficient time and life management, they can be applied to any, or all, aspects of our lives.

(1) Be absolutely committed to your learning and development

(discussed in more detail on pages 22 and 80). Companies are becoming ever more committed to *organisational* learning and development. This is hardly surprising when you consider that the companies at technology's cutting edge (such as those involved in the computer, telecommunications and pharmaceutical industries) assume that much of their technical knowledge will be out of date in less than a decade. The twin ideas of 'knowledge management' and being a 'learning organisation' reflect the growing need for companies to develop and implement that intellectual capital more effectively. Similarly, but on a personal level, you need to develop and implement your knowledge and experience, which means using time more effectively and creatively.

(2) Become a creative learner

Increasingly, creativity is the key to success. You may need to think creatively to find ways to overcome the problems currently facing you. And you need to be creative to adapt and implement the time and life management strategies outlined in this book to your particular circumstances. Many companies now value creativity above all other attributes (this is explored further in Chapter 7), but you can apply your creativity only if you are familiar with the current state of knowledge in your areas of interest.

Of course, creativity is about more than being a poet, painter or novelist. The psychologist Abraham Maslow pointed out in *Toward a Psychology of Being* that some people are creative outside the conventionally 'arty' areas. One of his women patients, for example, was 'original, novel, ingenious, unexpected, inventive' in the way that she cooked and furnished her home. He writes: 'I learned from her and others like her that a first-rate soup is more creative than a second-rate painting, and that, generally, cooking or parenthood or making a home could be creative while poetry need not be; it could be uncreative.'

Indeed, we all have the potential to be creative in many areas of our lives, but we need the time to explore these avenues. In some cases, these creative hobbies may even turn into careers. In this way, being a creative learner allows us to work towards our true ambitions. However, this relies on our freeing the time to determine and develop our potential.

(3) Envisage the future

Many companies now use a technique called 'visioning' to plan their direction and forge a sense of purpose. As we will see in Chapter 4, you can use visioning to imagine your future and give your life a sense of purpose that is in line with your core values and philosophies. However, it is important that both companies and individuals regularly review their progress.

(4) Form support groups

As a society, we live increasingly insular lives. Our families may be fragmented across the country, or even across the world, and few of us have large circles of friends. Yet, numerous studies show the benefits we can derive from the support of family, friends and neighbours. Indeed, the human race is naturally social.

At work, for example, people intuitively form support groups – often around the coffee machine. However, some companies now encourage more formal groups to exchange ideas and case histories. SOPHIE,★ for example, is a support group for secretaries and personal assistants working in drug companies. They meet regularly to exchange ideas and discuss best practice methods, as well as to stay

18

up to date with industry developments. If you work from home, you could try the Internet for similar work-related groups. Many free e-zines exist, including those that aim to help people with, for example, living frugally or simplifying their lives (see resources).

Companies increasingly recognise that a lack of support contributes to stress and undermines productivity. For example, at least 1,000 UK companies now offer workplace counselling to around 700,000 employees, covering issues as diverse as legal, relationship and work problems. While the workplace service is confidential, the counsellors can feed back recurrent issues, problems and concerns to senior management. Alternatively, you could consider seeing a private coun-sellor. Apart from helping you keep your problems in perspective, a counsellor can often show you how to develop problem-solving strategies. For more information contact the British Association of Counselling.★

(5) Marginalise your dependency on the organisation

However much you earn, for most people it never seems enough. Indeed, as Trix Webber notes, 'Most of us live up to our income and living below our means would require a significant, psychological and practical adjustment.' But you *can* make this adjustment (see Chapters 8 and 9) and without necessarily living in austerity. You will need to be prudent with your hard-earned cash, however, and that means breaking the cycle of earning and then spending as soon as, or even before, you receive your wages.

Being prudent also minimises your dependency on the organis-ation you work for. Obviously, if you are financially less dependent on your employer you have more options should you lose your job, opt for a career change or decide to set up your own business. Being prudent also reduces tension within the family, as worrying about bills is a leading cause of stress (in some cases, even more so than breaking up a relationship or arguing with your boss). In other words, being prudent is one important factor that helps put you in control of your life and your time. Indeed, living more frugally and within budget may even enrich your life.

(6) Give loyalty appropriately

When you are loyal to an organisation, be that at work or in the community, you agree to spend your time in its service. Therefore, your loyalty is a resource, just as much as your time or money, and you need to use it to your maximum benefit. Once again, this means working in line with your values and philosophy (see Chapter 4). Most people's first loyalty is to themselves and their families. Nevertheless, there is still a need to balance the various demands on your loyalty from work, family and yourself. Managing your time effectively is probably the best way to achieve balance among competing loyalties. The idea of opportunity costs (see below) offers a powerful way to think about the balance.

For example, although the job for life has gone, ironically, many companies now require greater commitment (another word for loyalty) from their employees than before. Twenty years ago, the average working week was 40 hours. Today, it is between 45 and 50 hours. We also commute further and for longer: 30 minutes on average 20 years ago, 55 minutes on average today. These changes swing the balance of loyalty in your company's favour. Therefore, in turn, you might wish to rethink your loyalty to the organisation for which you work. You may, for example, decide that you need to swing the balance back towards favouring yourself or your family by saying no to further demands from work.

It is important to realise that rethinking the balance is not the same as being *disloyal*. Rather, rethinking the balance of your loyalties means remembering that you have aims and priorities as well. As Webber points out, giving your loyalty appropriately minimises your dependency on the organisation.

(7) Have realistic expectations of organisations

Rethinking your priorities, commitments and loyalties in line with your views and philosophy releases your energy to develop skills that you will need to reach your life goals. Certainly, you need to look to the future, which is one reason why you should consider a skills audit (see page 80) and invest your time in life-long learning. You can no longer expect a company to look after you in an economic downturn. However, by investing time now in keeping your skills up to date and regularly thinking about your career path, you should be able cope better with any unforeseen potholes.

Few of us can expect a smooth journey along our career path. Downsizing and redundancy are unpleasant facts of life, even in the professions. Companies exist to maximise their profits and pay returns to shareholders, not to look after their employees. There are many enlightened companies and managers, but the harsh economic realities limit what you can expect from your employer, or indeed any organisation.

(8) Be politically aware

The pace of change in the modern world means that, more than ever before, you need to stay in touch with political and economic developments. Being politically aware allows you to act rapidly in response to changing conditions. Financial planning is one example. It is clear that to avoid subsistence living in old age, you need to make private pension provision (see *The Which? Guide to Pensions*, available from Which? Books).* However, a worrying number of people still rely solely on the state. Make time to keep track of your finances (see Chapters 8 and 9) and remain aware of socio-political trends.

(9) Develop your negotiating capacity

Traditionally, people like sales managers, reps, freelancers and those running small businesses needed to be effective negotiators. Today, *all* employees need to develop negotiating skills – to get the best remuneration package, for example, or to decline an unreasonable demand on their time. Later in the book, we will look at ways in which you can boost your self-esteem (see Chapter 5), overcome shyness and use a technique called 'transactional analysis' (see Chapter 3) to negotiate with other people. Transactional analysis also offers you new insights into the motivations of the people around you, who may impose considerable demands on your time, not to mention cause you stress.

(10) Intrapreneurial and entrepreneurial career-planning

If one thing is clear within the employment field, it is that traditional career and life paths are breaking down. Today, we need to take a broader view than our mothers and fathers. We have to cut our own paths through the employment jungle, rather than following in the footsteps of others. This means we may need to be intrapreneurs and entrepreneurs at different stages in our careers. An intrapreneur is innovative within a company, whereas an entrepreneur sets up a new company to develop an innovation.

In other words, you may need at some point to carve a new niche within the company in which you work. Later in your life, this may not be enough and you may decide to set up on your own. This means deciding what matters to you and determining how you can balance the competing demands on your time. Chapter 4 examines this in much more detail.

Learning is for life

In many ways, life-long learning – or, to give it a different spin, personal development – represents one common theme of these survive-and-thrive strategies. You may need to learn more about the political and financial culture to prepare yourself to meet the demands that you and your company will face. You may need to learn more about yourself and the opportunities that are open to you to plan your career. You may need to learn new skills, including those of time and life management. The world is changing so rapidly that no school or college course can prepare us fully for the paths that our lives and careers may take.

However, life-long learning means that you need to commit time to your development, to ensure success at work and in other parts of your life. If you do not like learning for its own sake, think of it as an investment. The time you invest now will yield a substantial return in the future. For example, your success at work depends to an ever greater extent on your unique skill set – in management-speak, 'what you bring to the party'. Employers buy this skill set. It is, after all, what sets you apart from your peers. To slip into management-speak again, it is sometimes referred to as your USP (unique selling proposition).

Increasingly, companies are looking beyond the narrow experience and expertise needed to meet a job description. In an interview with *Management Today* (July 1999), the president of Goldman Sachs, the international investment bank, noted that his company often looks for a broader skill base than simply experience in financial services. Siegmund Warburg, one of the industry's founders, hired people with 'a breadth of knowledge about the world, rather than a narrow business school focus ... and people who could write well and discuss history and other subjects.' This helps the organisation avoid institutionalising mediocrity. Even today, Goldman Sachs tries to recruit people from different academic, social and economic back-grounds. This means 'not, in effect, valuing credentials over character, intellect and disposition. And sometimes it means first hiring great talent – in some cases raw talent – then finding positions for them later.'

Such a policy is enlightened – and probably goes a long way to explaining the company's success. However, we can all take a leaf from its book by expanding our knowledge base. To do this, you may need to develop new skills and knowledge proactively, rather than just reactively keeping up-to-date in your narrow professional field. This should raise the value of your stock in today's competitive job market. However, it means you must ensure that you have enough time to invest in continual learning without throwing the rest of your life out of balance.

Personal development also means learning about yourself and your values. Although you will almost certainly find that your drive, motivation and ambitions alter (see Chapter 3) through your life, time and life management allows you to develop these forces to your full potential in line with life's changes.

If all this sounds like hard work, remember that life-long learning also increases your opportunities to relax and to explore your creativity. Being proactive (going out and doing something) is a more effective stress-buster than passively watching TV. Evening classes offer opportunities to learn anything from basket-weaving to Latin. So why not try something new?

Opportunity costs

Choosing how to extend our skills and enhance our lives leads to another core concept that you can bear in mind throughout the book: opportunity costs. Consider how you plan to make a big purchase without resorting to credit: you choose between the competing demands on your money. If you decide to spend money buying a new washing machine, you may need to put that weekend away on hold. In other words, the cost of the washing machine is the opportunity to go on holiday. Economists describe this as the opportunity cost.

A washing machine *versus* a weekend away may seem a trivial example, but the idea of opportunity cost underlies every aspect of time and money management in our 'cash-rich, time-poor' society. If you work late, you miss the opportunity to spend time with your children. If you decide to spend, as most of us do, four hours a day in front of the television, you miss the opportunity to spend that time gardening, learning French or writing that novel. Once we choose to do something now we forgo the opportunity to use that time on something else. It is an obvious concept, but one that we perhaps do not consider deeply.

Similarly, if you decide to become self-employed you may make a profit of £40,000 a year. However, if you could have earned £50,000 with an employer, the opportunity cost of your time is £10,000. It is important to realise that this does not tell you anything about whether the price is worth paying. Only you can decide whether it is worth losing £10,000 to work for yourself, for example.

When you look at an opportunity cost, try to take a comprehensive view. For example, when you decide to buy something, you forgo the opportunity to spend that money on something else. However, if you put the purchase on your credit card you need to be aware of the cost of borrowing: interest. This delays, rather than avoids, the need to make the choice. As Sarah Kennington, editor of the e-zine *The Frugal Life*,★ notes: 'Before I began living frugally, I never considered the amount of money that we were wasting on interest. It was nothing to charge $200 on a credit card for clothes. Now I would just about go in my birthday suit before I would do something like that. I'm doing everything I can to pay off any existing debt.'

Considering the opportunity cost is a powerful tool to help you balance your competing priorities and evaluate your life choices. What are you giving up to do this activity? In many cases, it is our families who pay the opportunity cost for our life choices. A 1999 survey commissioned by Abbey National exemplifies this. The survey found that four out of ten people said they could not spend enough time with their family and friends. A third were so pressurised that they forgot a relative's birthday or anniversary in the last year. In this case, our family and friends pay the opportunity cost for poor time and life management.

Similarly, the opportunity cost for over-commitment at work is the time that you could have spent on your hobbies or personal development. In the same survey, almost half those polled thought they were under too much pressure to go to the cinema, 36 per cent found no time to organise a holiday and a similar proportion were too harassed to garden. It seems that our health, families, hobbies, friends and relaxations are all part of the opportunity cost of a time-pressurised lifestyle. However, forsaking personal development can mean that you fall behind others competing for your job.

Making the choices can be hard. (We will look at some techniques to help you take decisions in Chapter 4.) However, it is worth remembering that, as the American philosopher Irving Singer pointed out, 'for everything we get in life, we must pay the price.' Only you can decide whether an opportunity cost is worth paying.

Empowerment: from the log cabin to the board room

Using the idea of opportunity cost can help us think about the consequences of our decisions and keep our lives balanced. In other words, it encourages us to make better-informed decisions. In fact, you could say that the idea of opportunity cost 'empowers' you to take life choices. Empowerment is something of a buzzword that has been rather devalued by repeated use. However, in essence it simply means taking responsibility for your life, choices and development.

Yet as the management researcher Pamela Johnson notes, many of us feel 'disempowered'. We feel passive and ineffectual in the face of increased demands from a changing world. As a result, many of us retreat within our shells to brood about 'long-lost dreams and missed opportunities'. Of course, everyone broods from time to time, but disempowered people feel chronically powerless and frustrated by the demands of daily life. This means that they become demotivated, and not just at work. The feeling of 'me against the world' can spill over into marriage and other relationships.

Locus of control
Psychologists describe disempowered people as having an 'external locus of control'. In other words, disempowered people see life as largely outside their personal control. Yet feeling in control is a major weapon in the battle against stress. Indeed, a company's most stressed-out employees tend to be those who are least empowered. They

are the workers who put in long hours for little pay and exert little control over their working lives: typically production-line workers, check-out assistants and people working in call centres. In contrast, while executive stress is a fashionable topic for magazine and newspaper articles, managers control their working lives to a much greater extent.

This feeling of disempowerment can produce mental and physical illness, and three studies illustrate this. The first study, carried out in Sweden, found that people who worked hard with little control over their lives consumed more tranquillisers than those who exert more control. The second study measured levels of cortisol, a stress hormone, in the pilots and co-pilots of a Japanese flight crew. The results, published in *Aviation, Space and Environmental Medicine*, showed greater variations in the co-pilots' cortisol levels depending on whether they were in control of the aeroplane. The pilots showed little change – probably because they are, ultimately, in control. This and other studies of air crew show that – even in highly stressful situations such as when flying – being in command is less stressful than accepting someone else's control.

Finally, in a paper published in 1999, researchers from St George's Hospital Medical School in London examined the link between job strain and psychiatric illness among 160 teachers. They split the teachers into two groups: those with high job strain, which they defined as highly demanding jobs with little control, and those with low job strain, typified by few demands and a high degree of control. Not surprisingly, they found that teachers under high job strain were more likely than those exposed to low strain to suffer severe anxiety, worry and fatigue.

Moreover, a feeling of helplessness in one area of a person's life often spills over into others. People who feel disempowered may, for example, feel unable to stop smoking, drinking too much or eating unhealthy food. Links between social class and illness are complex, but disempowerment certainly contributes to the association.

In contrast, empowerment, which time and life management aims to encourage, engenders an 'internal locus of control'. This seems to be the critical difference between people who try to tackle their problems and those who feel helpless. As time and life management is all about overcoming problems, you need to develop an internal locus of control. However, success tends to breed success. As you are able to control your time and overcome problems, you will feel more and more confident that you have an internal locus of control. In turn, this means that you are better able to control your time and overcome problems.

People who are empowered find it easier to adapt to changes. They begin to see that many aspects of their work and environment are within their control and realise that there is a close link between their behaviour and what happens. Indeed, you have to recognise this cause-and-effect relationship before you will be able to change your behaviour. Time and life management techniques aim to help you control the work around you, rather than allowing the work to control you. As such, they can help you become empowered.

To take one example: at some point in your life you have probably been told to learn from your mistakes and you probably have done so. But people with an external locus of control do not learn from their mistakes. Instead, they blame the failures on someone else. The failure to deliver a report was due to the train strike or the competing demands from a boss. Empowerment, on the other hand, means taking responsibility for your mistakes, as well as your successes.

Increasingly, companies are recognising the value of an empowered workforce. Empowered employees, Pamela Johnson notes, are willing to take on more responsibilities. They want to be innovative and creative. They are willing to take risks. Of course, from a manager's perspective this means that you may need to give up some of your power. But empowered employees tend to be more self-reliant, and that frees your time to handle other tasks.

Living deliberately

Although empowerment is something of a buzzword, the idea of living deliberately – which is really what empowerment is all about – is nothing new. Henry David Thoreau, born in 1817 in Massachusetts, lived for two years in a log cabin on the shores of a small lake surrounded by a wood, with strawberries, cherries and blackberries growing wild in his front yard. The book of his experiences, *Walden*, published in 1854, found few readers before his death eight years later. However, perhaps Thoreau was born a century-and-a-half too early, for *Walden* is now a favourite text of people trying to simplify and control their lives.

Thoreau describes how he simplified his life and reorganised his priorities to become what we would now describe as 'an empowered person with an internal locus of control'. In *Walden* he writes: 'I went to the woods because I wished to live deliberately, to front only the essential facts of life, and see if I could not learn what it had to teach, and not, when I came to die, discover that I had not lived. I wanted to live deep and suck out all the marrow of life.'

The key word is 'deliberately'. While living in a rural idyll may sound tempting, few of us can, or would in reality want to, make such a jump. But Thoreau's philosophy of living deliberately and getting all you can from life applies whether you live in a log cabin or in an executive home, whether you work collecting berries or in a boardroom. Everyone has to make choices, and those choices should be made deliberately. It is a way to enrich your life. And that is what time and life management is all about.

Chapter 2

Why time and life management isn't just for yuppies

Living as we do in a changing world, with commitments, hopes, dreams and ambitions, almost everyone can benefit from applying some of the principles of time and life management. Indeed, using the time and life management strategies, tricks and techniques outlined in this book could save you several hours a week. What you do with this time is up to you.

Eric

Eric knew he was unfit and a couple of stones overweight. He wanted to go jogging, but, as a busy marketing manager, he never seemed to find the time. He solved this by blocking off an hour in his diary each Monday, Wednesday, Thursday and Sunday evening. Eric refused to let anything – other than a real crisis – impinge on that time. Eric looked at time and life management as part of the self-discipline he needed to exercise. And he needed that will power, especially on cold winter evenings, not to be waylaid by the demands of work, spouse and children. He has now lost the excess weight and plans to run the London Marathon.

This chapter explores why time and life management is not just for yuppies. It begins with the archetypal yuppie disease – workaholism – and one of its major symptoms, uncontrolled spending. However, workaholism and its associated symptoms can affect people from all walks of life.

We then look at some of the problems faced by women at all

levels in the workplace who have thrown the pervasive lack of balance between work and family commitments in modern society into sharp focus. (For years, many men simply ignored the fact that their lives were unbalanced.) We go on to take a look at time management from the perspective of the elderly. As a society, we are living longer and that gives us more retirement time. Time and life management can help you to get the most from the retirement years.

Finally, we explore why managers need to manage themselves before others. This overview sets the scene for the time and life planning techniques outlined in the rest of the book.

Slipping into workaholism

As Eric found, greater self-discipline, which is another way of describing an internal locus of control, is another useful side effect of time and life management. If you order your life at home or work, you will be better able to cope with the new demands placed upon you.

Certainly, today's companies expect more than ever before from their employees. Indeed, workaholism almost seems to be a neccessary requirement for fulfilling some job descriptions. The idea of a nine-to-five job is dead for many of us. Almost a third of senior full-time employees in the UK work more than 46 hours a week. Senior managers often work more than 51 hours. This makes it easy to slip into workaholism – especially as many other changes in the workplace engender a sense of insecurity and many corporate cultures encourage, overtly or implicitly, workaholism.

On the other hand, some people *want* to work in high-pressure jobs that require a constant struggle against deadlines. They find that just reaching their deadlines produces an adrenaline buzz – almost a high. Therefore, some workaholics are, undoubtedly, satisfied and productive. Ironically, because they are constantly struggling against deadlines, they are often among the most effective time managers. They are able, if only out of necessity, to focus on what really matters to get the job done. While this might be fine if you are single and in a job you enjoy, if these circumstances change, this pressurised lifestyle can become a recipe for burnout.

However, while it seems to be self-evident that you get more done if you work longer hours, that is not necessarily the case. In fact, by working longer rather than smarter, productivity may even decline. Moreover, in some cases working long hours can be a symptom of an underlying psychological problem. A growing body of evidence links workaholism with other addictions. These studies suggest that, just like drug addicts or alcoholics, workaholics obsessively drive themselves towards their own destruction. Fortunately, time and life management can help slow the slide into workaholism.

What is a workaholic – and are you suffering from workaholism?

Essentially, a workaholic is driven to work excessively and obsessively in order to overcome inner tension. However, there are three main types of workaholic: those who work long hours to alleviate a feeling of anxiety; those who are perfectionists; and those who see workaholism as a way to attain their life goals.

Working to alleviate anxiety

Some workaholics find that working excessively and obsessively alleviates anxiety and stress. These feelings of stress come about either through the impact of environmental factors – pressure from your boss, for example – or internally, because of anxiety, depression or an impulse control disorder.

People suffering from impulse control disorders develop patterns of abnormal behaviour that can emerge as kleptomania (compulsive stealing), eating disorders (such as bulimia and anorexia), alcoholism or workaholism. However, whatever the outward manifestations, people suffering from impulse control disorders suffer growing anxiety that dissipates only when they engage in certain behaviours. Some workaholics, for example, feel a sense of growing anxiety that drives them to work longer and longer hours. In the short term, this alleviates the anxiety. However, the impact on their families often produces feelings of guilt and their lack of hobbies produces frustration, which triggers anxiety again. These people are true work addicts. Fortunately, a combination of drug therapy and psychological treatments can help such people take control of their lives again. (If you feel that you may be a true work addict, in the first instance talk to your GP.) Through time and life management, addicts can develop coping strategies to help prevent them from slipping back again.

Perfectionists

Some workaholics are perfectionists: they cannot finish a job until it is perfect. In some lines of work, being a perfectionist is a benefit: bank clerks and people drafting legal documents, for example. In other jobs, however, being a perfectionist is unnecessary or even impossible.

Goal-scoring workaholics

The third group of workaholics assume that they can attain their life goals only through workaholism. Many millionaires and politicians seem to fit in this group. However, perfectionists and millionaires-to-be still need to keep a sense of balance with other parts of their lives. There are numerous cases of people who gain great wealth, but whose family and personal lives are impoverished. The role of time and life management for each type of workaholic is to restore a balance.

The symptoms of workaholism

So how can you tell if you are a workaholic? Sometimes the workaholic is the last to realise. However, if your spouse or partner continually tells you that you are working excessive hours, then you probably are. Similarly, if you often feel guilty about the hours you work, then you may be working too much. Try keeping a log of the time you spend in the office and working at home. Then list your other commitments, including those you should or want to keep but are unable. You can then decide if your life is unbalanced.

You can also ask yourself if you suffer from the three hallmark symptoms of workaholism: firstly, being highly involved in your work; secondly, being highly driven or obsessive about your work to the detriment of other activities; thirdly, enjoying the feeling of working long hours and being under stress, or finding that working long hours alleviates stress and anxiety.

Most workaholics have high aspirations. If these aspirations are not realised, they feel dissatisfied. Indeed, this possibly contributes to some workaholics' pessimistic view of their prospects and careers. A 1999 study (published in *Career Development International*) of 530 managers and professionals found that workaholics tended to derive less satisfaction from their careers than other employees. They also believed that they had fewer prospects and were more likely to quit than their more balanced colleagues. (If these characteristics sound as if they could apply to you, the life management strategies outlined in the following chapters could help you get out of the career rut.) On the other hand, people who remain optimistic about the future are generally satisfied with their work and less likely to quit. The key is to do something that you love doing, while maintaining a balance with the rest of your life. This *is* possible and it is exactly what life management aims to achieve.

The vicious circle of time pressure and stress

It is not surprising that time pressures are a leading cause of stress. Most of us expect to feel stressed after a major life event, such as the death of a parent, losing our job or suffering from a serious illness. However, it is less well known that stress can creep up on us, arising from the cumulative impact of small challenges and problems. Yet, often we could have prepared for these, if only we had taken the time.

On the other hand, stress in itself is not necessarily a bad thing. A certain amount of stress is good for you, in fact. Stress describes our level of biological arousal. As we become more aroused, we release certain hormones into the blood, we mobilise energy reserves and our mental abilities increase – we become stressed, in other words. This means that there is an 'n'-shaped link between the level of stress and performance (see diagram overleaf).

You need a certain amount of stress even to crawl out of bed in the morning and deal with the trials and tribulations of modern life. As the pressure – stress by another, more socially acceptable name – increases, your arousal rises and your performance improves. Indeed, many actors and musicians welcome the stress of stage fright, which they know will enhance their performance. In fact, too little stress can lead to boredom and apathy, and can undermine concentration.

However, you can have too much of a good thing. Over-arousal, which is what most people mean by stress, undermines performance. At this point, you have passed the peak on the n-shaped curve. You feel stressed out when the demands on you outstrip your resources, strengths and, in particular, time. Around this point, your body will begin to tell you that you are overdoing it. So when physical or psychological symptoms emerge, when you begin drinking or spending excessively (see below), when your relationships at home suffer, you should rest.

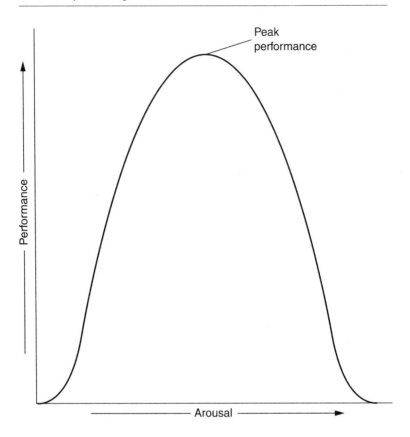

Peak performance

Performance

Arousal

Of course, many people do not heed their body's advice: they ignore the warning signs and begin burning the candle at both ends. If this is the case, you will feel on edge; and, indeed, you are teetering on the verge of burnout (see below). Your body is telling you to stop, slow down and take stock. But instead, you work longer and longer hours trying to compensate for your faltering productivity. Eventually, a small event may trigger a breakdown: you are burnt out.

While many people associate burnout with certain professions – stockbrokers, medics, teachers and so on – stress-related symptoms are far more common than you might suppose in all occupations. Around 10 per cent of the population experience emotional and physical ill health related to occupational stress, and about 7 per cent of GP consultations involve work-related stress. Against this background, the following quiz can help you decide just where you are on the n-shaped curve and whether you are at risk of burnout.

Quiz: Are you in danger of burnout?

Do you often feel stressed at work?	Yes / No
Do you often feel that you lack control over your work?	Yes / No
Do you often feel that you spend too much time working?	Yes / No
Do you often feel guilty about the impact on your family?	Yes / No
Do you frequently cancel personal appointments because of work commitments?	Yes / No
Do you often feel overstretched at work?	Yes / No
Do you fully understand what is expected of you at work?	Yes / No
Does your partner or spouse often complain that you work too much?	Yes / No
Do you often feel that you have too much work?	Yes / No
In general, do you feel you have too much responsibility?	Yes / No
In general, do you feel that you lack concentration?	Yes / No
In general, is your timekeeping poor?	Yes / No
In general, is your productivity low?	Yes / No
Do you often have difficulty understanding new methods and procedures?	Yes / No
Do you often feel irritable?	Yes / No
Do you often feel aggressive?	Yes / No
Do you often try to avoid working and co-operating with other people?	Yes / No
Do you often withdraw from social interactions at work?	Yes / No
Do you often resent your work colleagues?	Yes / No
Has your smoking or alcohol consumption increased in the last few months?	Yes / No
Do you often suffer from any of the following symptoms:	
Tiredness?	Yes / No
Excessive sweating?	Yes / No
Fainting?	Yes / No
Choking?	Yes / No
Breathlessness?	Yes / No
Nervousness?	Yes / No
Sleeplessness?	Yes / No
Muscle tension?	Yes / No
Headaches?	Yes / No

The more 'yes' answers, the more likely you are to suffer from work-related stress – and the further you are towards the right on the n-shaped curve. In other words, the more times that you answered yes, the closer you are to burnout and the sooner you need to do something about it.

When the going gets tough

When the going gets tough, the tough frequently stay at home. Research from the Industrial Society published in February 2000 revealed that managers blame stress and low motivation for much absenteeism. However, the survey, *Maximising Attendance*, highlights certain discrepancies between the employees' stated reasons and the managers' beliefs.

According to the survey, absent employees said that colds and flu, stomach upsets and headaches or migraines were the commonest reasons for taking time off work. Managers tended to agree that colds and flu were the commonest cause of absenteeism, but believed that stress, emotional and personal problems, as well as the 'Monday morning blues', were the next most common causes of absenteeism.

However, the distinction between stress and physical illness is not as clear as this might suggest: stress and cold symptoms seem to be intertwined. In 1991, researchers placed drops containing one of five respiratory viruses up the noses of otherwise healthy volunteers and then exposed them to varying levels of stress. The risk of contracting the infections rose with increasing levels of stress from 74 to 90 per cent, and the risk of catching a cold rose from 27 to 47 per cent. Again, the risk of infection rose with increasing levels of stress.

Such studies help us to understand the causes of absenteeism, which is clearly a waste of time for the company and often puts even greater pressure on the employee when he or she returns to work. Absenteeism is estimated to cost the UK economy around £13 billion a year. On average, each employee takes 8 days 'off sick' each year. Such figures not only imply logistical problems for companies and industries, but also indicate that, for many of us, our lives are unbalanced.

Steps to reduce absenteeism

The Industrial Society suggests that companies could take various steps to reduce absenteeism.

- Organisations should develop a policy on absence and monitor levels of sick leave. The policy should help diagnose the causes of absenteeism and find appropriate solutions.
- Companies should specifically train managers in the causes of, and most effective ways to manage, absenteeism.
- Companies should train employees to recognise and manage signs of stress. (You could use the burnout quiz on page 35.) Moreover, line managers should regularly consult and communicate with their staff.
- Improve motivation by providing employees with sufficient training and development opportunities.
- Managers should also ensure that employees are aware of their contribution to the business.
- Managers can use return-to-work interviews and informal procedures to keep individuals well informed and problems should be mutually resolved.
- Consider flexible annual leave, occasional working from home and, in particular, flexible working hours.

Many of these suggestions dovetail with the ideas central to time and life management. Unreasonable deadlines are, for example, are a considerable cause of stress and, therefore, absenteeism. Moreover, personal development plans that look beyond the office (see Chapter 4) empower employees and improve motivation.

Spend, spend, spend

Time and money are inexorably linked, and poor time and life management is a leading cause of stress. An increasing number of people now look to 'retail therapy', as well as to alcohol and drug abuse, in the hope of countering stress. The spend–spend–spend habit is one that is especially difficult to manage, in part because of the advertising industry, which entices us to spend from the cradle to the grave. In many cases, advertising is designed to create demand, irrespective of whether the product satisfies the consumer's genuine needs or not. To make matters worse, credit is easier than ever to obtain. Indeed, society seems geared towards encouraging us to earn more to spend more to reflect our social status. Inevitably, consumer debt rises to meet this created demand.

Certainly, spending offers some relief in the short term, and there is nothing wrong with wanting to surround yourself with useful or beautiful things. But again, it means keeping a sense of perspective. A spend-spend-spend lifestyle runs counter to many of the philosophies of good time and life management as well as those needed to survive and thrive in the modern world.

Excessive consumption increases your dependency on organisations, for example. It limits your options in the future and may even influence your career choices. Do you want that promotion because it helps you move towards your life goals or because you need the money to fund your lifestyle? As you move up the corporate ladder, you will probably find that you need to spend more and more time at work. Only you can decide whether this an opportunity cost (page 23) that is worth paying. Fundamentally, it remains debatable whether greater consumption makes us any happier at all.

The rapid growth in consumer credit has helped fuel this explosion in consumerism. Indeed, the first UK credit card, Barclaycard, introduced in 1966, transformed the way in which Britain spent its money. Thirty years after its introduction, a quarter of the population possessed a credit card, which accounted for almost a fifth of consumer borrowing, excluding mortgages. Many people have more than one credit card now, and the number of people with more than one card is growing. We spend over £1,000 *every second* on credit card transactions, and the average purchase is around £45. This figure, too, is likely to rise dramatically over the next few years with the growth of e-commerce. Around half the users pay off the balance each month. The rest pay a heavy price in interest rates.

Despite the ease with which most of us can now obtain credit, there is growing disillusionment with the spend-spend-spend lifestyle. Independent research commissioned by VSO★ found that 94 per cent of the people interviewed believe that Britain is becoming more materialistic, while 84 per cent said that we are under too much pressure to spend. As time and money management are so closely linked, ways to manage money more effectively are explored further in Chapter 9.

Compulsive spending

For some people retail therapy develops into a very serious problem. As impulse control problems underlie many cases of both excessive shopping and workaholism, some people suffer from both conditions. In other cases, acute stress can lead to anxiety and depression. And some people find that retail therapy eases their psychological burden. However, it is easy to become caught in a cycle of compulsive, even addictive, shopping.

Depending on what you consider compulsive, between 2 and 8 per cent of us are shopaholics. While the typical shopaholic is a woman, many men also spend compulsively. However, there tend to be differences in male and female spending patterns. Women shopaholics usually buy clothing, make-up and smaller items for the home. Men often go for electronic goods, sporting equipment, car accessories and so on. But for male and female shopaholics alike, the urge to spend is difficult to resist.

However, psychiatrists suggest that if you are frequently preoccupied with buying, if you often buy things you do not need or really want, if you usually spend more than you can afford, and if you often spend more time down the shops than you intend, you may have a problem. Of course, we all do some of these things to some extent some of the time. But people who shop compulsively act in this way most of the time and their preoccupation with shopping disrupts their daily life.

Like many psychiatric conditions, compulsive shopping is a question of degree. If you shop excessively each weekend and at lunchtime, you might well have a problem (most shopaholics shop two or three times a week). Some people need an emotional upset, such as a row with their partner or work problems, to trigger a buying binge. However, retail therapy offers only temporary relief from stress and anxiety. Away from the shops, shopaholics feel empty, agitated or anxious. Shopping produces a rush of excitement, although this high soon turns to exhaustion and depression.

Frequent shopping can also lead to considerable debt. In an American study released in 2000, the average shopaholic was around

£14,000 in debt, excluding their mortgage. However, the debt can reach £40,000, £70,000 or even more. Inevitably, the size of the debt, the problem of juggling credit and store cards, as well as the need to take out bank loans to cover the repayments leads to distress and guilt, especially among low or average earners. Obviously, the financial juggling that goes hand in hand with excessive spending also wastes a great deal of time.

So, how can you tell if you have a problem with compulsive spending? Answering the following questions should help.

Quiz: Are you a compulsive shopper?

Do you always or often shop alone?	Yes/No
Do you get a buzz or feel 'high' when you shop?	Yes/No
Do you often spend to relieve feelings of anxiety or depression?	Yes/No
Do you often spend when you are stressed?	Yes/No
Do you often spend after a row at home or at work?	Yes/No
Do you often buy things that you already own?	Yes/No
Do you often buy things that you don't need?	Yes/No
Do you often buy clothes without trying them on?	Yes/No
Do you have the same item of clothing in different colours?	Yes/No
Do you often buy clothes and shoes you never wear?	Yes/No
Do you often buy books you never read?	Yes/No
Do you buy CDs you never play?	Yes/No
Do you often carry a wallet full of credit cards?	Yes/No
Do you spend up to the limit on those cards?	Yes/No
Do you hide things that you have bought?	Yes/No
Do you lie about how much you have spent?	Yes/No
Do you want to impress other people with your purchases?	Yes/No
Is shopping your main hobby?	Yes/No
Do you ignore credit card and other bills?	Yes/No
Are you unable to window-shop?	Yes/No

The more times you answered 'yes' the more likely it is that you are a compulsive spender or even a shopaholic. True shopaholics are addicts and may need professional help. (Again, see your GP in the first instance.) However, if you think that you may be a compulsive shopper, try jotting down your feelings when you shop and examine the factors that trigger spending sprees. Once you have identified your triggers you will be in a position to do something about them (using, for example, the problem-solving techniques outlined in Chapter 4).

For example, if you find you spend more when you are alone, shop only with your friends or family. Ask their opinion about everything you buy. If you find you buy on impulse, try to wait a couple of days if you see something you want to buy. You can also shop with cash alone. Finally, compulsive and other impulse control disorders (see below) are symptoms of poor self-esteem. So you could try some of this book's tips on boosting self-esteem (see pages 110–11).

Impulse control disorders

Excessive compulsive shopping is one problem that can arise from an inner drive to work long hours or under pressure because of poor time and life management. Indeed, impulse control disorders underlie some cases of workaholism and shopaholism, although in other people an impulse control disorder may lead to alcohol abuse, gambling or taking drugs. Similarly, stress arising from, among other triggers, poor time and life management may also lead to drink, drugs and other problems.

Such problems seem almost commonplace. Around seven million British people drink more than the safe level, for example. In other words, around one person in six over the age of 15 drinks excessively. Of the four million people who are heavy drinkers, a quarter will suffer ill effects on their health as a result.

Indeed, people with impulse control problems can become addicted to almost anything, including the Internet (see page 166) and even 'non-addictive' prescription medicines, such as hormone replacement therapy. In the case of addiction to hormone replacement therapy, the women find that taking HRT keeps depression and anxiety at bay. While HRT can improve mood and help prevent heart disease and osteoporosis (brittle bones), the addiction is not a pharmacological effect. In other words, it is not an addiction in the same way as being hooked on heroin or nicotine; rather, it is an expression of internal torment.

All these impulse control disorders share common features: the addiction offers a quick fix for alleviating anxiety. But the person soon suffers withdrawal symptoms and is driven to repeat the experience, which simply makes matters worse. Indeed, most of these conditions mean that you have to work harder and harder to stay on top, both financially and more generally, as the addiction begins to dominate your life. Time and life management can help break the cycle. Freeing yourself, if only to a degree, from the ties that bind you to this cycle should allow you to begin to solve your problems.

Nevertheless, compulsive spending poses a particularly difficult problem. Spending is socially acceptable. Indeed, it is one way in which we show our status to the world. As a result, it is an activity that we all indulge in to a greater or lesser extent. So, as discussed in Chapter 1, most of us live up to our income. However, many people find that, ironically, living more frugally, well within their means, enriches their lives. More effective time and life management helps you achieve this.

Apart from looking at your bank balance, there are some other ways of telling whether your life is unbalanced and if you are in danger of becoming a workaholic and, therefore, teetering on the brink of burnout. At the end of each day for a typical week or two, answer these questions (adapted from *Family Practice Management*, March 1997★):

Quiz: Are you on the brink of burnout?

Do you feel tired all day?	Yes / No
Did you look forward to going to work today?	Yes / No
Has your day's work left you emotionally drained?	Yes / No
Did you feel in control of your time today?	Yes / No
Have you brought work-related problems home with you?	Yes / No
How confident do you feel about the future?	Yes / No
Did you lose your temper over minor things today?	Yes / No
Were the goals you set for yourself today realistic?	Yes / No
Did you find it difficult to concentrate?	Yes / No
Are you able to laugh at yourself?	Yes / No
Are you having difficulty relaxing?	Yes / No
Did you feel you had a strong support system?	Yes / No
Did you have more responsibility today than you can comfortably handle?	Yes / No

Were you able to say no when asked to meet unrealistic demands?	Yes / No
Did you have trouble making decisions?	Yes / No
Were you satisfied with the day's work?	Yes / No
Did you have difficulty getting to sleep last night?	Yes / No
Did you feel well organised today?	Yes / No
Do you feel pessimistic?	Yes / No
Do you feel in control of your personal life?	Yes / No

It is worth answering these questions once a day for several days, because if you pick a day at random it may not be typical. (A difficult day often triggers you to look at your life.) Indeed, American psychologists found that managers' attitudes towards their jobs varied dramatically even *during* the day. Indeed, the more closely you are involved in your work, the greater the variation through the day. Nevertheless, the more times you answer 'yes' to the above questions the closer you are to the brink of burnout.

This quiz could also highlight some particular areas you might want to work on. For example, if you have difficulty sleeping three or four nights, try some sleep hygiene tips (see page 118). Fatigue is one of effective time and life management's worst enemies. You could also note what you were doing that day. This might reveal, for example, that your worst days are those in which you have to meet your manager, deal with sales figures or meet a deadline. If you know what the triggers are, you can see where your stresses lie and develop a way to overcome them. The problem-solving strategies in Chapter 4, as well as the time and life management at work techniques in Chapter 7, should help.

Time and life management beats burnout

In essence, the main way to beat burnout is easy to say, more difficult to implement. You need to take time out for yourself. It means breaking that cycle of working harder and harder for longer and longer. Remember the idea of opportunity costs? If you choose to work longer hours, the opportunity cost is the time you cannot spend with your family or on your hobbies. This imbalance leaves you vulnerable to burnout.

Taking time out might be tough when you face deadlines, especially if you work for yourself or on commission, when time really is money. In reality, many of us have to put some extra hours in from time to time to meet work demands. In such cases, you can make an agreement with yourself: if you meet this deadline, you will take some time off next week. Note this time in your diary and stick to it – unless a *real* crisis arises.

Indeed, beating burnout, especially if you have a full diary, means scheduling rest and relaxation in the same way that you schedule a meeting. And stick to it. For example, some people hold their weekends as sacred and never work. This is their non-negotiable time. While this is difficult in some jobs, the principle applies to all of us. Mark the time off in your diary or planner and do not let anything – short of a real crisis at work or home – interfere with this time.

This means planning your leisure time in advance. Note in your diary (you should only have one – see Chapter 5) the days out you want to have with your family. Similarly, book your gym appointments well in advance, as cancelling is harder than not having to pick up the phone at the end of a tough day. Moreover, physical exercise is a real stress-buster and enhancer of performance. Also, make sure you take your holiday entitlement. Many people, especially those who work for themselves, book their next holiday almost as soon as they return from one. It is all too easy to let other matters encroach on the time you should take off.

You can also take time out during the day. Most computers now offer games such as solitaire and mine-sweeper as part of the package. A quick game can help reduce stress. Alternatively, try doing the crossword over coffee. Or look at a chess problem on a portable set. Taking a couple of breaks during the day is not wasting time. Breaks reduce stress and, therefore, enhance your productivity. Finally, use some of the tips in the rest of the book – especially those about delegation and saying no. Together, these approaches should pull you back from the brink of burnout.

Dealing with information overload

Finally, there is another trend facing everyone at home and work. We all have to master a vast and growing amount of information. Today, we have an unprecedented choice of television channels, web sites, newspapers, magazines and books. It is simply impossible to stay on top of every piece of information that matters to you either at home or at work, even if you work in a relatively narrow field. You will always have a lingering feeling that you might have missed that key item of information that could mean the difference between success and failure. Yet creative learning and being politically aware (which, as previously mentioned, are important in order to survive and thrive in a changing world), as well as staying on top of your job and your finances, mean using this information.

As a result, it is perhaps not surprising that information overload poses a growing problem. Over half the 5,000 executives interviewed for a 1999 survey by the Institute of Management said that they suffered from information overload, for example. To make matters worse, we live in the age of the sound bite, the executive summary and the bullet point. Increasingly, companies measure success not only in terms of expertise and performance *per se*, but in terms of how quickly you respond. In many areas of life, not just politics, deep analysis seems to have been replaced by the sound bite.

The information revolution contributes to this trend. The Internet links over 60 million people in thousands of organisations across the world. The World Wide Web contains more than eight million web sites connected through the Internet and continues to grow daily. Today, you can link to more than 900 million Web pages worldwide. How many you will find useful is another matter. It is often difficult to separate the informative wheat from the electronic chaff. Chapter 7 offers some suggestions to help you cope with information in the office. With a bit of imagination, you may be able to adapt some of these for the home.

The information overload also extends to consumer choice. Remember all those brands of dental floss mentioned in the first chapter? Visit any supermarket and think about the choice of breakfast cereal, biscuits and crisps. The choice can be bewildering. The key is to focus on what you actually need. All this excessive choice aims to tempt you, but usually only to spend money on something you neither want nor need. All too often, you pay the price with your time, your money and your health.

Balance business, family and personal commitments

Most of us want to balance our business, family and personal commitments. Effective time and life management is your main tool for restoring a sense of balance to your life.

Huw Jones, Vice-President and Managing Director of the UK arm of Élan (an international pharmaceutical company), balances his hectic lifestyle by following some basic principles. For example, he advises: 'Always take your holidays and avoid working weekends.' He also believes variety to be the spice of life. 'Give your brain something totally different to do for a part of your leisure time,' he suggests. 'A busy brain needs to stay busy so give it something lateral to employ it. But indulge the child in you at least once a week. Having young kids always helps. Play with them!'

However, while many men want to spend more time with the families, the problem posed by an imbalanced life is especially acute for women. Women's importance in the workplace continues to grow. Yet, despite the strides towards sexual equality over the last 20 years, most women remain primarily responsible for the home and childcare. This places terrific demands on women's time and life management.

Women's importance in the workplace

The days when women were destined for jobs as receptionists, nurses and secretaries before being married off are long gone. In 1996, 52 per cent of new solicitors were women, as were 32 per cent of managers and administrators, 34 per cent of health professionals and 27 per cent of buyers, brokers and sales representatives. Despite their growing importance in the workplace, the perception that it is women, rather than men, who need to meet their family commitments has helped reinforce the glass ceiling still found in many companies.

The result, as observed by Sharon Mavin, writing in *Career Development International*, is that 'women's career development does not simply lag behind that of men, but may proceed in a completely different manner'. She notes, for example, that the traditional working pattern – education, full-time career and retirement – applies only for men (although it is beginning to break down even here).

Traditionally, you climb the career ladder, gaining more responsibility the higher you climb. However, this path has never been the traditional one for women. Many women 'step off the fast track to meet family responsibilities', Mavin remarks. So some employers regard women as casual labour, and assume that they want a job only until they marry and have children. A feeling persists among male managers that even career women (the term itself is illuminating – whoever heard of a career man?) might quit work in favour of family responsibilities. This attitude might sound antiquated, but it is a perception that still often inhibits women's career prospects.

A survey by the Institute of Directors, for example, found that 45 per cent of its members regard women of child-bearing age as a less attractive employment prospect than other groups. Indeed, women currently account for only around 15 per cent of UK managers and less than 5 per cent of directors. Women still tend to earn less than men, are offered fewer promotions and tend to focus on specialist support roles – typically human resources – rather than central line management. Management consultants use the term 'glass walls' to describe this narrow career path.

Moreover, discrimination begins almost as soon as women start work. A 1997 survey found that the starting salary for women graduates was some 16 per cent lower than that of men with the same qualifications. Also, twice as many men as women enrolled on graduate training programmes. Even in America, the birthplace of the equal rights movement, highly qualified female managers – those holding Masters in Business Administration degrees – earn, on average, less than males. Furthermore, alongside age, gender is frequently cited by women as a significant impediment to career advancement.

Against this background, it is not surprising that many women feel disempowered, stressed and dissatisfied. Indeed, a survey carried out in 1999 suggested that working mothers are society's most dissatisfied group – which probably reflects the problems of juggling a job and family commitments, as well as the institutional, implicit discrimination at work.

Overcoming these prejudices will mean a major shift in society's and employers' attitudes. However, the fact that women have not followed the traditional career path may, ironically, prepare them better for the future than the ladder climbed by many men. Indeed, men could learn much from the way women manage their careers and lives in the face of these problems.

Breaking through the glass ceiling

The traditional difficulty of breaking through the glass ceiling may partly explain why women are more likely than men to regard their careers as a way to advance their personal development rather than to acquire conventional status symbols. The psychologist Jane Sturges found that women tend to regard career progression as a set of challenges, rather than thinking in terms of steps, goal or ladders. In particular, women are more likely than traditional male workers to look for interesting and challenging jobs that allow them to remain in balance with the rest of their lives (which is the aim of life management).

This means that women may be better prepared than men for the new world of work. The career ladder is starting to be pulled away from under the feet of many men, which suggests that men increasingly need to redesign their career and life plans along the lines traditionally followed by women. As noted in Chapter 1, taking a broader view of a career path is a key way of dealing with the uncertainties thrown up by the modern world. (Chapter 4 explores some ways that might help you gain this broader perspective.)

You are never too old to reclaim your life

Finally, you might think that time and life management is really for the young. But you would be wrong. For the first time in human history, most of us can expect to live to a reasonable 'old' age. A death before our allotted three-score-years-and-ten now seems a tragedy rather than a commonplace. To be sure, our physical and mental functions decline as we age. We might be able to slow the decline but, nevertheless, ageing sets limits on our aspirations, while, of course, death remains the inevitable ultimate limit. However, as Thomas Cole notes in his seminal book *The Journey of Life*, 'Human freedom and vitality lie in choosing to live well within these limits, even as we struggle against them.' Indeed, he points out that older people may experience 'higher peaks and greater depths' than younger people 'that *enrich reality* in later life'. Time and life management can help you experience this enriched reality.

On the other hand, you need to accept that your attitude to life changes as you get older. That is true even of the typical executive – the career climber (see Chapter 4) who in the early and middle years of his (for they usually are men) career sees success in terms of wage, car size and other status symbols. In later life, they come to regard influence and autonomy as more important than money or their position on the ladder. In part, of course, this is because they have already achieved financial or hierarchical success. However, it may also reflect changing priorities as we age.

Nevertheless, it is never too late to reclaim your time – and your life. There are numerous stories of people beginning the work that made them famous only in middle age or beyond. George Eliot's first published fiction, *Scenes from Clerical Life*, did not appear until she was 38 years old. Ian Fleming began writing his first novel at 43 years of age. That book, *Casino Royale*, started the James Bond industry. Brahms completed his first symphony at the same age. And William de Morgan led a successful career as an Arts-and-Crafts potter until the age of 66. Then he felt depressed, and friends suggested writing as therapy. The resulting novel, *Joseph Vance*, became a best-seller. Over the following nineteen years, de Morgan published eight more novels. These and many other cases show that it is never too late to teach an old dog new tricks.

Retirement could, therefore, be a time of unprecedented opportunity. Certainly, the idea of a retirement age is relatively new and somewhat arbitrary. While farmers sometimes passed responsibility for the farm to the next generation before they died and others lived with their families, widespread retirement was introduced only at the start of the last century. The Government introduced the public pension scheme, and therefore set the retirement age, in 1908.

Nevertheless, more and more of us will need to find something to do between retirement and death. According to government estimates, a man born in 1962 can expect to live until he is 73 years of age and a woman to 78 years. Their sons and daughters born in 1996 can expect to live to 75 and 80 years of age respectively. However, this is an average. Some of us will live much longer. The Government expects that number of people who reach their 100th birthday will increase from 6,000 in 1996 to 39,000 in 2036 and 95,000 in 2066. By 2080, at least one person a year will reach their 116th birthday each year – these are people who are in their 30s today.

Because of these demographic changes, society will probably undergo a sea change in attitudes towards old age. The psychologist C.G. Jung noted in the 1930s that many patients found their life devoid of meaning or purpose as they got older. Yet today we are increasingly able to tackle the ailments of old age, from heart attacks to cancer and Alzheimer's disease. This means that you could spend twenty or more years in good health after you retire. Time and life management helps you make the most of these years.

Indeed, older people are now tending to search out meaning and purpose in later life. They may rediscover a hobby they never had time for when they needed to earn a living and bring up a family. They may turn to the church and voluntary work or even take a course with the Open University.* The very fact that they are not tied down to a routine dictated by the demands imposed by earning a living means that they have something of a blank canvas. Time and life management can give people the brushes with which to paint. If you want to write that novel or get your degree, you will still need to find the time in the midst of the routine tasks of daily life. (*The Which? Guide to an Active Retirement* from Which? Books* has advice on planning for a secure retirement and making the most of your later years.)

We live in exciting times. For the first time in human history, most people can expect to live well beyond what we now accept to be 'middle' age. It is an opportunity that is too good to miss.

Managers, manage yourselves – before others

Now a word of warning for managers: manage yourself before you manage others. Of course, as a manager your success depends on maximising your staff's productivity, partly by encouraging effective time and life management. However, that means leading by example. As Niccolò Machiavelli noted some 500 years ago: 'Nothing makes a prince so much esteemed as the undertaking of great enterprises and the setting of a noble example in his own person.' That advice applies to time and life management just as much as to great business enterprises.

Beyond leadership

More recently, the American management guru James Scarnati described attributes that managers need to develop which go beyond leadership. For example, to survive and thrive we need to be able to monitor changes in our world and adapt appropriately. In other words, you need to be flexible enough to consider things from every angle and to adapt creatively.

Scarnati notes how the US Army teaches recruits that there is no simple formula that allows people to meet the challenges posed by every situation. Rather, it suggests that you remain 'flexible and attempt to gather as many facts as the circumstances will allow before you make a decision'. Ways to examine problems and overcome procrastination are covered in Chapter 4, and ways to boost your creativity are suggested in Chapter 7. You may need to be creative to implement the time and life management at work strategies outlined in Chapter 7 within the boundaries set by your company's corporate culture.

Scarnati argues that you need to back your creative, flexible approach with three other principles. Firstly, you should aim to display moral courage – in other words, stand up for your beliefs. However, this means developing and understanding your values and principles. (Some ways by which you can define these are covered in Chapter 4.) You can then consider your position carefully. If you still believe you are right, stand your ground.

Compromising your position is not necessarily the easy way out. It can lead to internal tension and discord, another leading cause of stress. On the other hand, if you decide to stand your ground, do so with tact and diplomacy. There are many ways to tackle problems short of outright confrontation. The techniques of transactional analysis (see Chapter 4) may help.

Secondly, you need to accept responsibility for your actions. This is obviously part of standing your ground, as well as being part of the price for being an innovator. As Winston Churchill said: 'The price of greatness is responsibility.' Of course, the best-laid plans of mice and managers often go astray, and trying to cover up mistakes may not be the best strategy. Being found out later may carry more serious consequences, as well as wasting more of your time. Moreover, accepting responsibility helps develop trust between you and your staff.

Cultivate the art of influence

Finally, Scarnati suggests cultivating the art of influence. This differs from the traditional 'command and control' management style. As is mentioned below, a more 'feminine' approach may be more appropriate, while the 'command and control' management style may be a sign of insecurity. Effective leadership relies on persuasion rather than threats or using their position of authority. Again, transactional analysis (see Chapter 4) can help.

The fact that young women tend to rely on persuasion rather than threats may explain why they often make the best managers – according to an Industrial Society survey of 9,175 workers, published in 2000, who were asked to rate their colleagues' leadership abilities. Women team leaders and supervisors, under 35 years of age and working in the voluntary or public sector, were considered better than male and female colleagues in higher positions in their ability to:

- empower those closest to the job to take decisions
- encourage and support staff
- achieve the job's purpose
- develop people and teams
- set an example by their behaviour
- build relationships based on trust.

In contrast, the older managers – both male and female – tended to have more of a 'command and control' style.

Commenting on the results, Debra Allcock, Head of Campaigning at the Industrial Society, said: 'The findings indicate the changing nature of leadership, which requires a more flexible, collegiate and feminine approach. This approach is not restricted to women. Older male directors must change their tunes, if they do not want to be overtaken by young women who want to bring a fresh approach to leadership.'

Your use of time will benefit from this flexible, managerial style. A more empowered workforce, which is really what this new leadership style confers, is less likely to make unnecessary demands on you and your time. On the other hand, you can empower your staff by encouraging them to use good time and life management techniques. As a modern manager, you can be a role model for you staff and show them how to consider the broader picture, beyond rigid job descriptions.

Chapter 3

Understanding change

Chapters 1 and 2 underline the fact that everyone faces ever more, and ever-changing, demands on their time. The world, it seems, is changing faster than ever before, and many of the old certainties are rapidly disappearing. Restoring balance in our lives benefits not only our companies but also each of us as individuals. Coping with the pressures imposed by the changing world means empowering yourself and, if you are a manager, your staff.

This means that you will probably need to change the way you manage time, yourself, your family and your staff. However, change is very stressful. Indeed, leading companies employ management consultants to help lessen its impact. The outcome of change may be beneficial, but the process can be traumatic. For this reason, this chapter explores the ways in which we decide to change and maps out the path you will need to follow as you try to implement your decisions about managing your time and life. It also offers you a map allowing you to plan your road to change, while the following chapter will explore how you can decide on your destination.

The dynamics of change

The map-drawing process is a powerful life management tool. It is used by, among others, psychiatrists, psychologists and management consultants. Its wide utility reflects the fact that the pathway applies whether you just want, for example, to organise your office better, quit smoking or downshift to that smallholding in the country you always wanted. Only the details and the speed at which you travel differ.

The way of drawing this map has been subjected to intensive research by psychologists to discover how and why we decide to change our lives. Understanding the dynamics that underlie behavioural changes should encourage people to change their diet, for example, or take up regular exercise, or even quit smoking.

Most of us know that being several stones overweight, being unfit or smoking is bad for our health. And many people who are unfit, overweight or addicted to smoking want to change. Indeed, some 70 per cent of smokers want to quit. In some cases, they will be able to change their bad habits through willpower alone. In other words, they will travel along the path rapidly, with little external motivation. Others, however, are able to go only so far before they slip back into their old ways. It may be that they will need to set off on the path several times before finally giving up their bad habits. Others still seem incapable of even starting down the road.

To explore the differences between people who can alter their behaviour and those who cannot, psychologists use the so-called 'Transtheoretical Model of Change', shown in the diagram below. Also called the 'Stages of Change' model, this tool helps you understand the processes you will need to go through before you

The stages of change

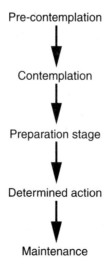

Pre-contemplation

Contemplation

Preparation stage

Determined action

Maintenance

make any behavioural or time and life management change, whether large or small. The 'Stages of Change' model applies just as much to a major change in the way you work as to giving up a bad habit, implementing some time and life management techniques or changing the way you shop. Appreciating where you are on this path as you try to tackle a problem should help you work out how you can move forward.

Trigger points

A trigger precedes every change, large or small. Think back to some habit you changed. You can probably identify a trigger. In some cases, a particular event prompts you to change. For example, someone who has always resisted eating a healthy diet may comply willingly after a heart attack. In cases of rapid change, people move very quickly through the stages outlined in the diagram. In essence, they jump directly from the pre-contemplation stage to the maintenance stage. However, many people find that they have problems *maintaining* the changed behaviour. More commonly, people change at a slower pace. They move gradually through the stages.

The pre-contemplation stage

At first, you are not interested in changing – even if it is for your own good. Psychologists call this the pre-contemplation stage, when you are often in denial. Drinkers deny that they have a problem with alcohol, for example. People who are overweight deny that they need to lose weight, despite the evidence facing them each morning in the mirror. Someone who is struggling, unproductive and continually on the brink of chaos because of their poor time and life management may think that they are fine 'just muddling along'.

Often, however, the denial hides a feeling of disempowerment. During the precontemplation stage many people have, subconsciously at least, an external locus of control (see page 25). Nevertheless, eventually something happens – or the evidence simply becomes overwhelming – and you realise that something had better change. Some heavy drinkers wake up one morning and realise that they have to stop. Others need to be confronted at work or at home before they take steps to control their alcohol consumption. Ideally, you should act on your initiative, rather than waiting until your boss confronts you with the evidence of your poor time and life management during your annual appraisal, for example. The fact that you are reading this book suggests that you recognise this. However, if a problem at work or home prompted you to examine time and life management it is probably best to tackle this first.

Whatever the trigger, once you realise that you have a problem you move into the contemplation stage. This is the first step towards becoming empowered and taking control of your life. During the contemplation and preparation stages, you move towards making the change and taking control of your life.

Moving towards change

During the contemplation stage you may not really know whether you want to make the change. Often giving up a behavioural pattern leads to a sense of loss that can be difficult to overcome. Moreover, at this stage, there always appear to be numerous barriers to break through.

For example, a long-term drinker may wonder how he or she will fill the hours that were previously spent drinking or manage in social situations without a drink to bolster self-confidence. Perhaps the chaos at work furnishes you with an excuse for why things are late or not performed to the best of your ability – after all, you might tell yourself, you were snowed under with work. Or perhaps you fear failure. That is why you never go on that diet, try to run a marathon or pick up the brush and paint the way you always wanted.

In other words, the contemplation stage offers you an opportunity to take a long, hard look at the pros and cons of the change that you are considering. This means taking the idea of lifelong learning to heart and determining to discover all you can about the pertinent issue. You may, for example, want to understand better the risks associated with smoking and look at the various techniques that can help you quit. Or perhaps you want to start an investment fund for your children's educational fees or for your retirement. If this is the case, look at all the different options available and discuss them with an independent investment adviser.

Asking yourself two key questions can help during the contemplation phase. Firstly, ask yourself, 'What would it take for me to change?' This may uncover the factors motivating you to change. For instance, a smoker could ask: 'What would it take for me to quit? A diagnosis of cancer or heart disease? Recognising how much money I spend each week on my nicotine addiction?'

Secondly, consider the other side. What are the barriers and problems that stop you from making the change? What currently stops you smoking or putting away money each month towards a nest egg? What are you afraid of? Critically, you need to ask yourself what you get, or used to get, from your current behaviour.

However, in many cases, you may not be able quite to put your finger on what is holding you back or presenting the obstacle. So try brainstorming: list *everything* you feel *could* hold you back. Do not make any judgements about these factors at this stage. List everything, no matter how silly it may appear. Then strike out the things you can do nothing about: age, physical illnesses and so on. Next, strike out the factors that are impractical, perhaps for financial reasons. You will then be left with the barriers and obstacles that fall within your control.

Understanding the problem

The next step is to explore these barriers and obstacles, and find a way to solve the problems facing you. On a blank piece of paper, try answering the following questions.

What is the problem?

Try to state the problem in a clear, simple sentence: 'I can't meet my deadline for the monthly sales report three times out of four.' 'I can't control my drinking.' 'Often I buy things I don't need.' If you cannot state the problem in a simple sentence, you may have more than one problem. So try breaking the problem down. You can also hone in on the fundamental problem by considering what the problem is *not* or the circumstances in which it arises. 'My spending is under control, unless I row with my boss,' for example.

Who contributes to the problem?

List all the people who influence the problem, for good or ill. Then consider who makes matters worse and who helps. The American self-help writer Richard Carlson also suggests asking yourself: 'What have I contributed to this problem?' Most of us lay the blame for problems at the feet of other people. However, frequently we have at least contributed to the difficulty.

Where does the problem occur?

At home? At work? Many smokers and people who either drink (or eat) excessively respond to environmental and emotional 'cues'. Their drinking may be well controlled most of the time, but in social occasions, at parties, or when they are away on business they drink excessively. Some people eat to comfort themselves. Understanding where a problem occurs can help uncover some of the reasons *why* it occurs.

When does the problem occur?

Similarly, looking at *when* a problem occurs can help you understand some of the reasons why it occurs. Is there a time in the month when two or three imminent reports mean that you are pushed? Keeping a diary may help reveal when and where a problem occurs.

Why does the problem occur?

Look at the answers to the above. Some patterns and, hence, appropriate solutions may emerge. Again, brainstorming helps you look at the possible solutions, however silly and however expensive. You could ask yourself, if you had your time over again or in an ideal world, what would you do differently? Now consider your best options? Which can you afford? The person who drinks to bolster self-confidence may need assertiveness training, or may need to boost his or her self-esteem, for example. You could tackle the problem of the multiple reports by trying to spread certain parts, such as information-gathering, throughout the month. You might also be able to produce a rough draft, which you can update with topical figures later.

If the problem affects several people or departments – such as at work, for example – you could ask as many of the interested parties as possible about the problem and find out their suggested solutions. Listing these may indicate a number of common approaches. You could then take this a step further by asking your colleagues to number the three or four that seem best, in order of preference. While this does not allow you to abdicate your responsibility for taking the final decision, it shows that you have been proactive at gathering other views and may suggest solutions you have not considered. Sometimes finding an answer to disagreement, which lies at the heart of many problems at work, does not mean seeking agreement. Rather it means learning to live with each other and learning to benefit from other perspectives.

These questions should reveal some ways in which you can overcome the problem and move to the next stage in the dynamics of change model. We will look at the steps to implementation, which essentially involves setting long-, medium- and short-term goals, in Chapter 4.

If all this fails

If you still cannot identify the time or life management problem or find a solution might want to consider seeing a counsellor. Counsellors are experts at suggesting ways to solve life's problems. But bear in mind that if you ask yourself these questions first, you might gain more from the consultations. However, often we have made such a large investment in some of the factors contributing to a problem that it can be hard to see the wood for the trees. An outside view often helps.

Counsellors also help if the problem lies *within* you. The poet T.S. Eliot said that life's problems fall into two types. For the first, you can ask: 'What are we going to do about it?' For the second, you need to ask: 'What does it mean?' and 'How do we relate to it?' Most time and life management techniques help you answer the first type of question, while answers to the second type of problem lie more in the realms of religion or metaphysics. Most people suffer a 'spiritual crisis' at some time during their life – for example, following the death of a loved one. In such cases a counsellor, priest or teacher may help. Nevertheless, working out your personal values and philosophy (see Chapter 4) and using techniques such as mediation, t'ai chi and yoga (see Chapters 6 and 9) show how to explore these deeper issues.

Cast off your baggage

A holistic approach allows us to take a long, hard look at our problems. Also, the contemplation phase of the dynamics of change model allows us to cast off some of the historical baggage that we all carry with us – or, at least, look at it in a new light. As Richard Carlson notes, the idea that the person we were yesterday is the same person that we are today and have to be tomorrow is 'one of the most severely limiting beliefs' that we have. He suggests reminding yourself that your life is behind you now. As the cliché goes, 'today is the first day of the rest of your life'.

Nevertheless, the past can cast a long shadow – for good or ill. We may look back at schooldays, the college years or a past career as the best time of our lives. However, as the American philosopher Irving Singer points out, we cannot restore 'those cherished goods of the past'. And ask yourself, would you really want to? As Singer argues, our position in life today, the opportunities that we can grasp and the challenges that we need to meet, is so *because* we have moved on from the time in our lives when we held these cherished goods in our hands. 'It was only in response to their loss that we could have acquired the possibilities present to us now,' Singer says. As we age, the chances are that we would no longer see those days in the same light now. All too often we view the past through rose-tinted glasses.

Indeed, we often act in accordance with what psychologists describe as a 'life script', laid down in childhood and largely written around our childish strategies and imagination. As we mature, this life script becomes buried deep in our subconscious, only to emerge at times of stress. For example, bereavement early in life can undermine self-esteem (see Chapter 4) and one's view of the past, present and future. This life script may mean that you selectively remember depressing or negative memories that fuel and maintain a negative view of life.

In such ways, our life script can make implementing any change – from simple time and life management to the larger changes needed to meet our life goals – extremely difficult. 'This inner nature rarely disappears or dies,' writes the psychologist Abraham Maslow. 'It persists underground, unconsciously, even though denied and repressed . . . it speaks softly but it will be heard, even in a distorted form.' In other words, your life script can undermine your attempts at change, whether that is a simple lifestyle modification or a more wide-ranging alteration.

On the other hand, a life script is not necessarily a bad thing. Our life script can reflect our true values, dreams and ideals. However, we often reject these values, dreams and ideals as we try to fit into the image of an 'average', 'successful', 'well-adjusted' adult. Indeed, we often regard these childhood dreams as 'dangerous'. As Maslow points out, turning your back on this part of the life script means rejecting much of what is fundamental to our nature. By such rejection, we lose touch with the sources of our joys and playfulness, as well as our ability to love, laugh and be creative. By protecting ourselves 'against the hell within', we also cut ourselves off from the 'heaven within'.

Reacting inappropriately

As we tend to read from our life script when we are stressed, it can lead to inappropriate reactions. For example, if you received sympathy when you were ill and cried as a child, then you may still react to stress by crying or developing psychosomatic symptoms (aches and pains with no physical cause). However, the reaction will have little relevance to your current situation. Try thinking back to a pertinent recent event.

- How did you react? Was it a childish response? Or was it a response worthy of a balanced adult?
- Did you experience inappropriate anger?
- Were you tearful, anxious or embarrassed?
- What trigger factors surrounded the event? Were you out of control? Did you fear failure or inadequacy?
- Are you still trying to live to expectations established by parents?

Understanding how you react to stress should help you stop wasting your time and your life with inappropriate responses, which necessitate picking up the pieces in the aftermath. Why react with anger to constructive criticism that you know in your heart is valid, for example? It will just hold back your personal development.

Reflecting on the past year and writing down moments that stand out to you, both good and bad, helps you understand your life script. You can take this a step further and consider the defining moments in your life. All of us face a series of major life choices that set us on course for the next few years – such as the choice of a job or partner. So, think about these moments when your life course could have gone one of two or more ways:

- Why did you choose one route over the other?
- How did you feel?
- Would you do anything different if you faced the same choice today?
- To what extent did other people – a spouse, parent or employee – influence the choice? While we are individuals in control of our lives, only the most selfish person would ignore their loved ones' wishes when considering a major life change.

The choices we make at these times define our character as well as reflecting our life script. Considering your life script – perhaps with the help of a counsellor or psychoanalyst (Chapter 4) – helps you understand the historical baggage you carry. Not all of this is unwanted on your life voyage. Some of it you want to keep. Other bits you can jettison. The process of change, evaluation and review outlined in this chapter helps you rewrite your life script and act more appropriately to current circumstances. As Maslow remarks, psychoanalysis (and some of the suggestions in this and the next chapter are a kind of do-it-yourself therapy) aims to heal the split between our internal heaven and hell.

After a period of reflection

Typically, people spend three or four months mentally chewing things over before they decide to prepare to make a life change. However, some people remain at this stage for years. By the preparation stage, you will have decided to make the change and will now be taking specific steps towards carrying out a plan of action, usually within the next month.

The preparation stage offers an ideal time to experiment with smaller changes, which give you confidence but are not enough to make a significant difference. Drinkers and smokers may try to avoid the cues that, in the past, led to binges or lighting up. The executive may try a few of the time and life management tips to see the benefits. This might entail keeping a diary or record of the impact. These small-scale experiments are important – they give you the confidence to move to the next bigger step. As Huw Jones, Vice-President and Managing Director of the UK arm of Élan Pharmaceuticals, comments: 'Give yourself something you know that you can do or win at – get into a positive spiral.'

In for the long haul

Once you have made some inroads with these smaller changes, you can then make the bigger alteration and take determined action to incorporate the new behaviour into your daily life. You then need to stick with it.

Many psychologists believe that it takes between three and six months to change a fundamental behaviour or habit. We all know how few New Year's resolutions are kept for more than a few days or weeks. A *Health Which?* survey in 1996, for example, found that, less than two weeks after they resolved to stop or cut down smoking, 40 per cent had already given up giving up. A third of those who resolved to lose weight had thrown in the towel, while almost a fifth of those who had resolved to reduce their alcohol consumption were actually drinking more.

Clearly, old habits die hard – as anyone who tried and failed to stop smoking or drinking knows. Relapses are common. You may start implementing time and life management changes and then find yourself overwhelmed again. When you are trying to make the most of your time and your life, an unexpected problem can undermine your efforts. Similarly, the average smoker takes four or five attempts to stop smoking successfully. A stressful day can lead to a smoker reaching for the packet or a drinker stopping off for a pint. It is hard when this happens to pick yourself up again. This means that you have to think of yourself as being in for the long haul. You may well slip. However, what matters is not to give up.

So, if you do slip up, it is important to perform a post-mortem to help prevent further relapses. Look at the reasons why you lapsed. Can you identify any triggers? Is there anything that you can do to prevent yourself from lapsing again? After several months, these new patterns of behaviour become the habit and your life changes for the better.

These stages of change offer you a road map for altering your behaviour and implementing time and life management techniques. Chapter 4 explores the ways in which you can decide where you are going. Otherwise, this map will be a road to nowhere. Unless you know your destination, you may never reach your full potential. As Robert Louis Stevenson suggested: 'To be what we are, and to become what we are capable of becoming, is the only end in life.'

Chapter 4

What really matters

As the earlier chapters of this book showed, there is little point improving your time and life management skills unless you know where it is you want to go. You may well travel faster, but you will still be on a road to nowhere. As already mentioned, leading management consultants to many of the world's largest corporations now recognise that helping employees restore a sense of balance in their lives improves productivity. Moreover, consultants counselling managers and executives suggest that to survive and thrive in today's world you need to look beyond conventional job descriptions and career plans. Therefore, this chapter examines how you can decide what you really want from life; it should also help you to clarify your attitudes and values.

Mark

'When my father died, I went through a period when I was terrified of my own mortality. Even though I was still in my mid-thirties, I felt that death was waiting just around the corner,' says Mark, an ex-management consultant who now runs a second-hand and antiquarian book business. 'It was an intensely distressing experience, but my mind began to focus on what really mattered to me. I'd laid the groundwork before, but his death and the realisation that, in the words of a cliché, life isn't a rehearsal, prompted me to put my life in order and to begin to do what I always wanted to. I needed to step off the fast track. But I feel it's sad that I needed my father's death to get my priorities sorted out. I should have done this years ago.'

Management gurus now tend to suggest that identifying life priorities is the key to time and life management. The rest then follows. However, how many of us know what we really want out of life? Few of us take the time to examine our lives, unless we face a crisis.

Mark, in the case history, is not alone. Many people have difficulty finding the time to discover and articulate their dreams, values and philosophy. Interviews with VSO* applicants and volunteers (see Chapter 1) show that our fast-moving, consumerist lifestyles do not allow us the time or space to assess our personal priorities. Moreover, media hype, advertising and the demands of modern life tend to distort our sense of what is important. But without finding the time, without making the effort, we may never reach our full potential. The time and life management techniques described later in the book can certainly make you more efficient and effective as well as reducing your stress at home and work. Yet, without focus, you will still have no idea of where you want to be and so will just go nowhere faster.

Even if you are a hard-nosed executive trying to play the management game by today's rules – which seem to have not just moved the goal posts, but changed the pitch and the shape of the ball – you may still need to work out your fundamental values and philosophy, then act in line with these. The management consultant James Scarnati observes that today's top managers need leadership attributes other than technical expertise. Firstly, executives need to display moral courage – the 'conviction and fortitude' to stand up for their beliefs. To do this, leaders need to develop the second attribute: a value system and set of principles relating to moral courage and ethical behaviour. This helps to develop a framework that will set you apart from your peers. As such, it can give you an advantage in an ever more competitive world.

Reclaim your life

Time and life management helps you reclaim your life, but that requires focus. This section helps you develop short-, medium- and long-term priorities that, together, take you towards your ultimate goal. The first step should take you about half an hour. However, the benefits could last a lifetime.

This process – which management consultants call 'visioneering' – allows you to understand and articulate your basic principles, values and philosophy. These core values act as the foundation upon which you take decisions that guide you towards your ultimate life goal. The more conventional time and life management tools described later in the book allow you to implement these decisions, effectively and efficiently. (The difference between efficacy and effectiveness is explored in Chapter 7.) As a result, your personality will begin to be expressed in everything you do.

Indeed, the decisions that you take and the choices that you make are the tools with which you can sculpt your life. The philosopher Mel Thompson suggests 'seeing your life as the material out of which, through the choices you make, you are gradually constructing a work of art . . . through your choices, you shape your life; you practise the art of living.'

The art of living

It is only recently that most people in the developed world have had the luxury of being able to consider the art of living. Our ancestors were too busy with the daily struggle for survival. It was this that formed their life goal, as indeed it still does for most of the world's population. First, we need food and water. Next, we need protection from predatory animals and other people. Then we need to feel a sense of belonging to a group that offers a way to meet our nutritional needs and protection. And once we belong, we need to feel valued by that group. We can think of ourselves and our self-fulfilment (also called self-actualisation) only once these needs are met. In the 1950s, Abraham Maslow described this as the hierarchy of needs (see figure).

Maslow's hierarchy of needs helps us understand our basic motivations. Today, most people in the developed world are adequately fed and watered; they have a reasonable degree of security; and they feel, to a greater or lesser extent, part of an affluent society. Although the UK still has a worrying number of marginalised people living in poverty, most of us now crave appreciation and self-fulfilment rather than food and shelter. Nevertheless, if you do not meet your needs for appreciation and self-fulfilment, you will feel unmotivated and dissatisfied.

Maslow's hierarchy of needs

In practice, life management helps you move up the hierarchy. Perhaps you feel that your job does not offer the financial security that you think you need (although it might be worth questioning the value of what more money will bring: things you really need, or things that merely allow you to keep up with the Joneses?). Perhaps you feel unappreciated or sense that you do not belong to your current social group. This chapter looks at some ways in which you can clarify your goals and explore your motivation. Indeed, you can think of this goal as the final product; the issues you will work out here as the plan; and the time and life management techniques (laid out later in the book) as the tools. While en route to your goal, you can use the management techniques to free the time to begin this voyage of self-discovery.

Deciding on your goals

You can use several strategies to help you understand and articulate your goals. For example, you could ask yourself these questions.

- If I could choose one thing to achieve before I die, what would it be?
- What are my professional goals over the next five years?
- What are my professional goals over the next year?
- What are my professional goals over the next month?
- What are my personal goals over the next five years?
- What are my personal goals over the next year?
- What are my personal goals over the next month?
- What are my family's goals over the next five years?
- What are my family's goals over the next year?
- What are my family's goals over the next month?

Another method is to write a 'wish list'. It does not matter how silly, trivial or unrealistic some of these wishes are. It does not matter if they are childhood fantasies or simply unattainable dreams. You can filter out the childish and obviously unattainable later, preferably after putting the list to one side for a couple of days. Of the wishes that are left, you will probably find that there are some that you can realise quickly, while others you can modify slightly.

Many of the other wishes will focus around some common themes. Try to rewrite these as specific ambitions: 'running the London Marathon' rather than 'getting fit', or 'being a size 12' rather than 'losing weight', for example. Next, place them in some sort of order – in terms of importance, for example. Thinking about common areas will help highlight your personal, professional and family goals.

However, such goals need to be consistent with your values. Consciously or not, these values helped shape your decisions throughout your life. Therefore, reflecting on your choices – the way they shaped your life and reflect your life script – helps define these values. We can learn from all our choices, whether we regret them or not, and considering our choices clarifies ways in which we can move forward.

For example, our careers, relationships and political views all reflect the values we held at one time or another. We may now regret some of these views – everything changes and our views evolve – but you need to stop activities that are inconsistent with your core values. Other values are more consistent and remain core to the way we see ourselves and the way in which we aim to lead our lives. These values need to be better integrated into our lives.

However, do not be too attached to your past prejudices and attitudes. As was noted in the last chapter, everyone changes and develops with age, so we need to embrace and welcome these modifications as evidence of our personal development. It shows that we are managing our lives. However, expect some people to think that you still adhere to your older views.

Your mission statement

Developing a personal mission statement helps you get in touch with your core values. Your company probably has a mission statement. Nike's is 'To experience the emotion of competition, winning and crushing competitors'. The technology giant 3M, which makes everything from drugs to Post-It notes, aims 'To solve unsolved problems innovatively', while Disney's exemplifies the mission statement at its simplest and most engaging: 'To make people happy.'

These mission statements are supposed to encapsulate the company's values and philosophy in a pithy phrase that engages the emotions of the staff, at all levels of the company. The mission statement offers a standard to which the company generally, and each member of staff individually, aspires. However, it has to be attainable and able to help each member of staff reach a goal, either personally or as part of a team, which they would be unable to do alone. Management gurus point to the cleaner at the Kennedy Space Center who, when asked what his job was, responded: 'I'm putting a man on the moon.'

To write a mission statement for your life, ask yourself what you want to achieve. What is the philosophy underpinning your life? Where do you want to be in five or ten years? This mission statement should also reflect the various roles you play: parent, spouse, employee and so on – as well as what you want to achieve in each of these domains. Once you have written down the answers, try to hone in on any common themes: perhaps it is 'to be the best you can be while staying in control and in balance'. Perhaps it is 'to make a difference to the lives of your family and the wider community'. Or, if you are self-employed, perhaps it is 'to work over the next three years to maintain or improve your business's competitiveness.'

The mission statement should help you align your behaviour with your beliefs – a theme we will return to repeatedly in this book. Many people either keep their mission statement in their personal organiser, on a card pinned over their desk or on their computer. This mission statement also offers you a vision of what you want to become. As American management guru James Scarnati comments: 'With vision comes direction, and with direction comes purpose, and with purpose comes commitment'.

Write it down

It is important to write your mission statement down. Indeed, it is better to perform most of the exercises outlined in this book on paper or screen. There is something about writing that makes your ambitions, ideas and hopes seem more concrete, more real. For example, Michael Heseltine planned his life on the back of an envelope as a student in Oxford. He might have failed in his ultimate aim of becoming prime minister, but he has still had a remarkably successful business and public life.

Writing can even be therapeutic. For example, psychologists use 'therapeutic writing' to help patients come to terms with suffering from physical or psychological illnesses, including cancer, depression and rheumatoid arthritis. For all of us, writing something down gives it a permanence and legitimacy it may otherwise lack. A written statement is also something you feel you can control. However, you need to be honest. No one will see this mission statement except you (unless you want them to – but think carefully before sharing it).

Writing your mission statement helps you get in touch with your inner ambitions, values and philosophies, all of which are frequently hidden behind layers of day-to-day cares and concerns. And you should listen to these inner voices. The Roman statesman Marcus Cicero pointed out that 'nobody can give you wiser advice than yourself'. However, that advice is valuable only if you are honest. For example, many people harbour a vague ambition to work for themselves, ideally at home. While it is tempting, you have to remember that working at home suits only some people. You need to be highly self-motivated, able to spend hours alone and to work outside a corporate culture. You must also be able to cope without the social and administrative support that a large company offers.

Other approaches

A number of other approaches can act like a key to unlock your aims and ambitions. One sobering approach is to write your own obituary – twice. Read a few obituaries in a quality newspaper and then write your ideal obituary, the way you would like to be remembered. As a good father? An excellent wife? Someone who worked hard for others? Now the tough part. Be honest, which is the hard part, and write your obituary as it would be today. Compare the two. How do they differ? What can you do to move from the second obituary towards the first?

The management consultant Brian Clegg suggests imagining you have won the lottery. Which current activities would you still perform? Which would you drop? What would you do with the money? This type of approach allows you to decide which of your current activities matter to you, and, in turn, this should offer some insight into your values. Unfettered by financial concerns, would you open a bookshop? Run a self-sufficient smallholding? Paint? This use of your imagination should also help you articulate your life ambition.

Finally, if you want to focus on your role at work, consider your role as a professional, a manager and a leader:

- the professional role is, obviously, the job you trained for – say, a doctor, accountant or teacher
- your role as a leader includes, according to the management writer John Adair, offering direction as well as inspiring, motivating and building a team
- your managerial role concerns the nuts-and-bolts of running a business from day to day, such as establishing systems and controlling finances.

Now imagine that it is your retirement day. How would you like to be remembered by your staff and managers? What contribution would you like to have made to the company in each of these three roles?

★

Whatever approach you choose, type or neatly write your mission statement, list your three or four core values, note down your ultimate ambition and keep this information to hand. When you need to make a key decision, when you need to examine your plans, this will help you decide whether your choices are in line with your philosophy and values, and whether they can take you towards your ultimate goal.

A broad approach brings business benefits

Fundamentally, these approaches have one thing in common: they allow you to examine the broader picture. Even hard-nosed executives are beginning to see the business benefits of taking a broader view, and are prepared to invest their profits in consultancy services that can facilitate this. A growing number of companies now use personal development plans rather than traditional job-focused appraisals. Personal development plans encourage staff to consider their performance in the context of their entire lives, relating performance to hopes, ambitions and expectations. In contrast, traditional appraisals track performance against narrow criteria defined by job descriptions. A personal development plan may, for example, cover job skills, the company's wider business aims, an employee's home and personal life, as well as that person's life within the general community.

Obviously, personal development plans benefit employers. Personal development plans offer employees a feeling of security in an insecure world. This reduces stress, a multi-billion-pound cause of absenteeism, and improves productivity. Moreover, looking beyond the workplace may reveal skills and a competency that the employer can harness.

Indeed, the psychologist Jane Sturges notes that developing flexible, portable, alternative career paths, which the personal development plans summarise, helps companies secure 'the motivation and commitment of an increasingly diverse workforce'. She notes that development programmes that do not reflect individual values and beliefs are unlikely to deliver the commitment and motivation needed to hone a modern company's competitive edge. You also benefit as an individual from working on a personal development plan. The process crystallises your life aims and moves ownership of your career from the company to you.

What motivates you?

Against this background, understanding your motivation is another important element of life management. You need to think about your basic values and philosophy when you come to plan the rest of your life. (This presupposes that you are at the top two or three levels of Maslow's hierarchy of needs – see page 67.) Moreover, considering what motivates you may help you thrive in the changing corporate world.

For example, traditionally we measure career success in terms of our position on the corporate ladder, as well as salary and bonuses, such as a company car. However, all that is changing, and most large companies are moving towards a flatter corporate structure. If the company has fewer middle-management layers, it is harder to define success in terms of a position. Similarly, there is a growing recognition that, to many people – especially among women and older workers (see below) – success means something different to hierarchical and financial status alone.

To understand your motivation better, you can think of yourself as an influencer, expert, self-realiser or climber – or, believe it or not, a character from *The Wizard of Oz*. To a certain extent, this sort of analysis is a game. I doubt if anyone fits exactly into these classifications, and, indeed, these broad characterisations probably apply to all of us to a certain extent. Nevertheless, they can help crystallise your motivations and identify issues that you may want to address using time and life management.

By way of an introduction, look at the factors that contribute to your ideas of success. Understanding these factors may help you work out *what matters to you* from your job. In fact, you could write down what you mean by success in terms of each of these categories. Then you will be better placed to work out how you will achieve these markers of success using your time and life management skills.

What constitutes success

The psychologist Jane Sturges asked a group of 36 managers to define what they mean by success. Many of their answers differed markedly from the conventional view. She classified these motivators into seven success criteria, which, to a certain extent, overlap.

Reward

For some managers, the pay and bonus package was the main success marker. However, other criteria played at least a supporting role, and most managers thought beyond their pay cheque to at least some extent. Indeed, most managers reported that some of the other six factors were far more important in their idea of success than pay. Obviously, however, this depends on being paid sufficient to meet the basic level for food, utilities and housing (see Maslow's hierarchy of needs on page 67).

Accomplishment

Some people need not only to feel that they are good at what they do but also that they are receiving recognition and confirmation for what they do. This confirmation can be simply be in terms of pay or status. For other managers, personal recognition could mean winning awards, attending a conference or even just being thanked. For others, success depends less on other people's approval. In such cases, accomplishment could mean obtaining a sense of personal achievement from the job, being regarded as an expert, or moving along a personal path towards an internal personal goal.

Personal achievement

Again, managers interpreted personal achievement in several ways. It could mean being a pioneer, cracking a difficult deal, being creative, or developing through their work.

Enjoyment

Work that is interesting and enjoyable is often satisfying. Even the most money- and status-focused managers wanted to enjoy their job. However, some people said that they would pass over the opportunity for promotion if it meant moving away from a job that they enjoyed. Certainly, it seems that enjoyment is essential for a balanced, satisfying work life. As the British novelist Samuel Butler noted: 'People are always good company when they are doing what they really enjoy.'

Integrity

The managers interviewed defined integrity as a feeling that their job is worthwhile; that they act with integrity; and that they are able to put something back into society. In general, managers' rising interest in organisations such as VSO,★ highlighted in Chapter 1, may reflect the growing significance attached to this success criterion. Moreover, many people feel that they should put something back into society and volunteer for anything from football practice to hospital radio or helping a charity. However, acting with integrity means understanding and acting in line with your values and philosophy. As Scarnati notes, executives need to develop a value system and set of principles that promote moral courage and ethical behaviour – the foundations of integrity.

Balance
A number of managers cited the balance between their home and work life as being important. Indeed, failing to maintain this balance can cause stress and ruin your quality of life. For example, a recent study found that young and middle-aged women were more stressed than older females. This reflects the pressure of juggling demands of their spouse, children, ageing parents with the demands imposed by their occupation, while trying to maintain inner balance. As proposed throughout this book, time and life management aims to help you restore a sense of balance in your life.

Influence
While, again, most of the managers interviewed wanted to be influential, influence means different things to different people. Indeed, for some, influence is the main factor driving their ambition. Money and status were just tools allowing them to exert more influence.

Climbers, experts, influencers and self-realisers

Based on her findings, Sturges described four types of manager, depending on the weight that those interviewed applied to each of the criteria. She called these types *influencers*, *experts*, *self-realisers* and *climbers*. Of course, we are all probably a mix of each of these. However, deciding which best describes your ambitions and philosophy should help you crystallise your life plan. Moreover, if you are a manager, thinking about your staff in this way should help you motivate and reward your team in the most appropriate way.

Firstly, *climbers* describe career success in the traditional terms of hierarchical promotion and financial reward – in particular, pay. However, status means more than just position on the corporate ladder. For climbers, status also means social success and status. As a result, climbers tend to be highly competitive and focused on goals and targets within their organisation, which they tend to view positively. Nevertheless, even among climbers, money alone is not enough to ensure a satisfying career. Climbers need to enjoy their work in order to feel successful. Typically, climbers are men in their twenties and thirties who thrive in corporate life.

The second group are what Sturges describes as *experts*. For experts, success means being – and, critically, also being seen to be – highly competent at their job. Rather than money or position, experts regard success in terms of being seen as knowledgeable, gaining positive feedback and thanks from their peers and superiors, as well as obtaining respect among their colleagues. While money and position are important, experts regard them as surrogates for their expert status rather than as things of intrinsic value. Most experts regard the job's content as more important than position within the company and they may pass on promotion as a result. Many engineers and scientists fall into this group.

The next group, the *influencers*, want to have a meaningful, tangible and positive effect on the company, and perhaps society more generally, irrespective of their position. Essentially, influencers want to leave their mark while attaining autonomy and responsibility. As a result, influencers value promotions because of the additional influence they can bring to bear. Many influencers tend to become involved in activities outside the narrow job description. Nevertheless, these people can be very ambitious, especially if they see promotion to the top of the company as the best way to wield the most influence.

Finally, *self-realisers* have an internal, personal view of success. They define success in no terms apart from their own. Indeed, in many cases their definitions would, at best, mean little or, at worst, be incomprehensible to an influencer, an expert, a climber or even another self-realiser. Indeed, many self-realisers have difficulty expressing just what they mean by success, especially in organisational terms, even to themselves. Nevertheless, their internal model of success underpins everything else they achieve: money, promotions, influence and so on. Indeed, it seems that self-realisers need work to be challenging and interesting on a personal level and any goals tend to be personal staging posts on their road to their ultimate aim. However, perhaps more than any other group, the self-realisers want to balance work, home and their lives in general.

To understand these differences, and to determine which apply to you (a task that should help you consider your life management options), imagine that an influencer, expert, self-realiser and a climber were at the same level in a corporation. The climber would regard the hierarchical status and the financial package that position offered as important *in themselves*. The influencer would value the position for the influence he or she could bring to bear, while the expert would regard it as a marker of the esteem his or her expertise had brought. The self-realiser would regard the position as an important staging post on the journey of personal development. However, the influencer, expert and self-realiser would judge the pay packet in terms of its utility rather than the status it might bring.

Now ask yourself which of the characterisations best describes your attitude to your current and previous positions? Thinking about these internal factors helps you understand what drives you. In turn, this should help you work out the best way to achieve your ambitions.

This does not mean that climbers are superficial, self-realisers too self-centred to be team players, or influencers power-crazy. On the surface, there may be very little difference between the success or commitment of influencers, experts, self-realisers and climbers. Nevertheless, each brings different strengths to a team. Perhaps contrary to what you might expect, just seven of the 36 managers Sturges interviewed were climbers.

Are you a cowardly lion?

The American management researcher Pamela Johnson uses a different paradigm − based on *The Wizard of Oz* − to help understand motivation. Again, thinking about yourself in these terms helps you plan your life management strategies.

Johnson describes workers as being 'Scarecrows', 'Tin Men' or 'Cowardly Lions'. In other words, the three 'keys to empowerment' are brains, a heart and courage. Without these, she argues, the workforce becomes 'passive and unmotivated'. On the other hand, developing these characteristics produces people who are 'less risk-averse, more creative, and more willing to suggest bolder solutions' – which is really what modern, broad-based time and life management aims to achieve.

Each of us has a bit of the Scarecrow, Tin Man or Cowardly Lion in us, which is probably why *The Wizard of Oz* is such an enduring story. As Johnson points out, the Scarecrow, Tinman and Cowardly Lion all feel vulnerable, and 'each is looking for empowerment and self-direction'. At times, all of us look 'for brains, a heart and, most of all, courage'. For example, for Scarecrows to become empowered, Johnson suggests replacing their negative, limiting attitudes with 'a fierce determination to reach their goals'. That means defining your goals, deciding how to accomplish them, and then 'just doing it'. Life coaches and work mentors can help – as can the techniques outlined in this book.

A Tin Man wants a heart. Johnson defines this as wanting 'psychological ownership'. From a business perspective, this means that everyone in an organisation shares a sense of responsibility for the company's actions and success. However, we also need heart in our lives generally. We need to follow Johnson's advice to find meaning in our daily tasks, to look beyond the pay cheque, to have a community or corporate spirit and just to have fun – or at least be enthusiastic.

Often this does not mean changing jobs or dropping out to live in a log cabin. It really means changing your attitude to the job or lifestyle you already have. Many time and life management techniques allow us to impose a greater degree of control over our increasingly hectic lives. As we manage to meet the demands imposed at work and home, we will be better able to see the meaning in our normal lives.

Finally, the Lion wanted courage. He felt powerless, depressed, angry and afraid. (This is a classic example of someone with an external locus of control – see Chapter 1.) You need to have guts to take responsibility for your actions, think positively and respond to whatever happens, viewing setbacks as challenges.

You could try comparing your current performance with these three criteria. Do you need brains, a heart or courage? Do you need to clarify your goals better to ensure that you are able to move up towards self-fulfilment (brains)? Do you need a job that fulfils your need to do something for others or that allows you to spend more time with your family (heart)? Or do you want to be more assertive at work, or start your own business (courage)?

What each of these terms means is really up to you. These and other ways of describing people are, in some ways, just tools offering you some insights into your life. However, they offer a different way of looking at your life and problems, which can be very illuminating.

Finding your courage

Of the three characteristics, finding your courage may be the most difficult. So when you next face a difficult challenge, how can you find the courage to move on? Some people suggest listing the worst scenario that can happen. They argue that this keeps fears in perspective. 'Figure out what you can manage, achieve or fix, and do it. And figure out what you cannot do anything about, and either ignore it or put it aside. Eventually you will forget about it,' says Huw Jones, Vice-President and Managing Director of Élan in the UK. 'Don't prevaricate . . . ask yourself: "What's the worst thing that can happen?" The answer is usually not as bad as you think.'

This approach suits many people. The problem is that some people catastrophise. They can make a seemingly logical – albeit extremely improbable – progression from saying 'no' to an unreasonable demand to losing their job and then their house and then their marriage. So, if you try thinking 'What's the worst that can happen?', keep your fantasies within reasonable bounds.

Another approach, advocated by the self-help author Richard Carlson, is to think, 'How much will this matter in a year's time?' If it will still matter, then you need to really consider it. However, think back to what you thought was a major issue or problem last year. Does it still matter? If so, what have you done to address it? Nevertheless, you will be amazed at how many seemingly pressing issues simply fade into insignificance.

Finally, overcome procrastination. Eventually you need to have the guts to take the plunge. It is worth testing your nerve with some smaller, less important issues. Once you have the courage to tackle these, then you are better placed to move on to the bigger problems.

The big picture

If you have followed the course of the book so far, you are probably now well versed in your motivations, values and attitudes, as well as having some insight into the problems you face and the ways to tackle them. You probably also have an idea of your ultimate ambition: become chair of the board; write for a living; work on a smallholding; whatever.

The next step is to identify some steps that move you along the road towards your ambition. You should break your journey into between three and seven key measurable stages. For example, if you want to live the 'good life' (becoming self-sufficient), some of the stages might be: learning about agriculture; working out a business plan; and choosing which part of the country you should move to. Of course, the three stages are intertwined.

Deconstructing the big picture helps you appreciate its constituent elements. Now set yourself a time to achieve each area of the big picture, based on the stages and the ultimate goal. After looking at the key areas, you may decide that five years is a realistic time scale. You can then set a time scale for each key area. You then break each of these down into medium-term objectives after performing a skills audit.

Audit your skills

During a skills audit, you look critically, but realistically, at your current situation in the light of your ultimate aim. You then decide which areas you need to improve in order to reach your goal. Based on this, you can set yourself medium- and short-term goals to improve your skills. However, it is essential to review your progress regularly. You can also use a skills audit to overcome particular problems at work – for example, if younger people are being promoted over your head because they can offer certain skills or knowledge.

Begin by listing your successes. You probably have many more options and skills than you think. Therefore, list:

- your educational qualifications
- your professional qualifications
- your interests, skills and knowledge – at work

- your interests, skills and knowledge – outside of work
- any awards you have won
- any courses you have attended
- your job history – and what you have learnt. Against each job you have held, try to figure out between three and six things that you have learnt, both as additions to your skill set and personally. Remember, even the worst job in the world allows you to add to your skill set and teaches you something new about the world
- what roles do you play outside work? Are you involved in the scouts? Or a local football team?

(This process is also invaluable if you are trying to put together a C.V.)

Now ask yourself how these can help you reach your ultimate goal. You should try to be creative. For example, if you are computer-literate but want to live on a smallholding, could you run an e-business to bolster your income? Could you sell rare breeds or a premium farm product over the Internet?

The audit should help you assess the skills you need. How far do your skills fall short in each key area? Perhaps, for example, you need more IT training. Then find out the ways in which you can address this need: training courses, books, distance learning and so on. For example, you could consider brushing up your academic skills with the Open University★ through an evening course, distance learning or books.

Next, break each skill shortage into short-, medium- and long-term goals. It is important to deal with one skill, task or problem at a time. Often people fail to change, not because they set their sights too high, but because they try to do too much too soon. So, you should set yourself clear, specific and achievable targets. These changes should be small enough to fit into your daily life once you implement the appropriate time and life management strategies. There is no point, for example, setting yourself an unachievable study programme. You are likely to fail, and obviously that will not engender a sense of success. On the other hand, succeeding in some of these smaller, short-term goals means that you will develop the confidence to take larger steps. So, break large projects into small, manageable parts. Any journey, however long, is made up of numerous small steps.

Moreover, you need to assess accurately the amount of time that each short-, medium- and long-term goal will take. Then add around 10 or 20 per cent to each estimate. Most people underestimate how long a task will take, especially if it is something they have not done before. You can find the time you need using some of the techniques outlined in this book.

Finally, review your progress regularly, perhaps once every three months. If you have achieved what you set out to do, reward yourself. However, you may have to be persistent and patient before you get to your ultimate aim. Some 121 publishers rejected Robert Pirsig's 1974 classic *Zen and the Art of Motorcycle Maintenance*. The 122nd accepted the book, which went on to sell over three million copies.

Take that decision

Some 2,000 years ago, the Roman historian and orator Cornelius Tacitus noted that: 'The desire for safety stands against every great and noble enterprise.' Two millennia later, it is still true that most of us need to cling to what we know, rather than take the plunge, even if that is what we really want. Eventually, after all this planning, after you attain your short- and medium-term goals, you are going to have to take the plunge and go for the ultimate aim. You may have to leave a relatively secure job. You may have to go for promotion. Yet taking that final step is not easy.

Even in our day-to-day lives, procrastination wastes time for many of us. And once procrastination becomes a habit, you create problems for yourself and for others. In the short-term, procrastination can make life easier – especially if the task seems daunting or unpleasant, you fear failure or you are a perfectionist. Underlying all this is an unspoken hope that, if you ignore the problem or task, it will go away. Yet, for success, both in business and in our personal lives, making the right decision at the right time is often vital. The key seems to be to get as much information as possible, evaluate it, and then take the plunge.

In a *Management Today* feature, Tony O'Reilly, Heinz's chairman, said: 'To me, the best way to make a decision in an imperfect world is to try to get as much information as possible about people, cost, personalities, potential – and your rivals – and then, make your decision.' In the same feature, Penny Hughes, a non-executive director with a number of leading companies, agreed. After gathering and assessing the best-quality information, she makes her decision and then corrects 'on the run'. She advocates this approach, rather than waiting until everything falls into place – principally, because things do not necessarily work out smoothly. 'Things are never perfect – you can never have a perfect understanding of complex issues.'

Sometimes taking a decision means knowing when to cut your losses. In many cases, our fear of stepping away from what we know means that we try rearranging the deckchairs on our personal *Titanic* instead of abandoning ship. We have invested 10 years of our life in a marriage that has clearly failed, thousands of pounds in a company that is failing, or years of commitment in a job we hate. Because we have made these investments, we keep sinking our resources to try to stay afloat. Psychologists call this the 'sunk cost fallacy'. In other words, an investment that needs further expenditure. You see the sunk cost fallacy played out in any casino: people who have lost money but cannot stop playing in the – usually vain – hope that they will recoup the money lost. Most people would advise the gambler to cut his or her losses. However, it is advice that few of us follow in our daily lives.

Against this background, avoiding procrastination means accepting a degree of uncertainty. Change is just about the only certainty today. Learning to deal with uncertainty can be difficult, but it is a key life management skill. Indeed, the more fluid and ambiguous the situation you face, the greater the degree of uncertainty you have to accept and deal with. On the other hand, the higher the degree of uncertainty, the more influence you can exert. Again, thinking about any problem in the light of the Stages of Change model (see Chapter 3) might help you move forward.

Peter

Deciding to take the plunge can be difficult. Peter Llewellyn is Founder and Managing Director of InPharm-Internet Services Ltd, a leading Internet company for the pharmaceutical industry. He was also one of the first people to dip his foot into the waters of the World Wide Web.

'Looking back to the early days of the development of InPharm, one has to understand that it was just three years ago when most folk weren't online, the dotcom explosion hadn't yet started and the Internet was truly uncharted waters, at least in the way we know it today. For a long time, I didn't really have any sort of a plan, just a belief that this new environment was worth exploring.'

However, Peter had already taken one tough decision – to start a medical communications agency, Maxim Medical. Peter's main drive was a desire to self-actualise, to reach his full potential. 'My thoughts at that stage about starting my own business were based on a desire for independence, wanting to control my activities and a willingness to take responsibility for those actions. With no family responsibilities, it was, at the time, a simple decision. I always felt I could go back to employment if I needed to. Meanwhile, why not give it a go?'

Peter admits that things were tough at first. 'The first year running Maxim Medical was tough, to put it mildly. I took on a small team of staff and hardly stopped to draw breath. I severely underestimated the constant pressure. There was simply no let-up. No boss to offload responsibility on to. Where were all those support staff I was used to in financial and administration departments and so on? However, it was great fun and it's amazing how much more open your mind can be when it isn't constrained by organisational issues and people politics.'

In the meantime, the Web's development caught Peter's imagination. 'I found that not having a boss suddenly meant I was free to pursue my own interests,' he says, and in 1998 Peter set up InPharm-Internet Services Ltd.

'It was a very different business to what I was used to,' Peter admits. 'So why did I do it? Simply because it seemed blindingly obvious to me that such a service was needed and no one else seemed to want to do it. One day I woke up and found I was spending most of my time developing the service without any clear reasoning behind it. I took a long hard look and decided it was worth trying to keep going. Again, having no restraining influences in the shape of family or boss helped.'

However, Peter admits that, at first, not everyone shared his vision. 'There was a huge degree of scepticism from people within the industry and more or less everything we did was for free. Almost immediately, we had success with some of the job ads we published within InPharm, but convincing anyone to pay anything for anything was near impossible. It was vital to me that Maxim Medical kept on going, in order for me to survive. So juggling the two businesses was now a seven-day-a-week project and a whole different level of pressure to what had gone before, which itself I had thought had been tough.' Apart from money, Peter made other sacrifices. 'A social life for one. And money – everything I had in the world at one stage was effectively gone,' he admits. 'And health, probably, too.'

Now Peter feels that his sacrifices have been worth it – a major scientific publishing company now backs the site. 'The kick comes from hearing people talk about us, acknowledging how far we have come and how valuable are the services we now run and the way the whole service is growing rapidly and effectively. And with the new investment comes a whole new level of opportunity to develop the business, but also to bring in the resources we need in order for me to back away a little and lead a more normal life.

'My advice to anyone thinking of developing their own ideas? Just do it, don't think about it,' he says. 'It is most likely going to be harder than you can imagine and the pressures are very individual – so no one can really advise you. We are all different in terms of our strengths and weaknesses and until you try you don't know. Ask yourself: what happens if I don't try? Never has there been a time when so much is possible. Working for yourself isn't going to suit everyone, though. In my experience, most folk know if the time is right for them. So, go in with your eyes open, but don't think too long about it. Life is too short.'

Chapter 5

The essential elements of time and life management

The techniques outlined in the last chapter should help you clarify your values, philosophies and ambitions as well as help you develop a plan for moving towards your final destination. Now you need to find the time to put your plan into action. This means maximising your effectiveness and efficiency at home and work. We will look at some specific suggestions to improve your time and life management at work and home over the next few chapters. However, all these rely on some essential elements of time and life management, explained in this chapter.

These essential elements lay the foundations of all time and life management systems, whether you use a powerful computer program or a simple paper list and diary. The choice is down to you and should reflect your needs. As we will see later in this chapter, modern computer programs and palmtops are powerful and, for many people, indispensable. However, you obviously need a computer to run these programs, they can be expensive and, for many people, a high-tech approach may be a management sledgehammer to crack a fragile time nut. They are invaluable for some people in some jobs – sales managers, executives, reps and so on – but you should think critically before you invest in such high-tech approaches.

Indeed, thinking critically and taking what is useful to you is, perhaps, one of the most important principles in time and life management. Despite what you may think from some books and courses, there are no rules in time and life management. Indeed, some of the most widely quoted time and life management 'rules' seem ideal in theory, but simply do not work in our day-to-day lives. This means that you need to hone your critical edge. Think about every piece of advice and see whether it applies to you. Ask yourself:

is this change really necessary? Is it worth the time and effort to implement? In most cases, the answer will be yes. However, asking yourself these questions will help you keep in mind the reasons behind your time and life management changes.

That said, the principles outlined in this chapter should offer a basic framework for improving your time and life management skills. You can then hang the specific techniques (outlined in Chapters 6–9) that work for you on this framework.

Where does the time go?

A business truism states that 20 per cent of the effort produces 80 per cent of the results. For example, about 80 per cent of your sales probably come from approximately 20 per cent of your customers. And in many cases, 80 per cent of your output comes from 20 per cent of your time. You can argue about the exact percentages. However, your aim should be to rewrite this equation so that you spend around 80 per cent of your time at home and at work on your priorities.

It is up to you to decide what these priorities are. Some business time and life management books and course set hard-and-fast rules, such as that only 15 per cent of your time should go on routine tasks, while you should spend perhaps 60 per cent on planning and development. Whether this applies to you depends on your job description: a person in quality assurance or production may need to spend most of their time on routine tasks. The 60 per cent ratio is more appropriate for people working in business planning or marketing strategy.

However, it might be worth deciding on your priorities, perhaps in discussion with your boss, and grouping these into broad categories. Then you can decide what proportion of your time you need to spend on each activity to meet your work commitments. However, before you can do this effectively, you need to know where the time goes, whether you are in an office or at home.

Performing a time audit

Performing a time audit is the most effective way to examine where your time goes, although it can be laborious and takes some self-discipline. However, it is worth making the effort because it tells you, for example, how you *really* spend your time, as opposed to how you think you spend your time. A time audit can show how a gradual accumulation of tasks and responsibilities can sneak up on you, lengthening your 'to do' list. Eventually, you begin to feel overwhelmed. Performing a time audit enhances your awareness of time and how you spend it.

Examining your present position is essential. Think about some tasks that you need to do over the next couple of weeks. Now estimate how long you think they will take and how long they *should* take in an ideal world. Revisit these estimates once you have performed the time audit. When you look at the results – and when you look at your financial situation (see Chapter 9) – try not to become too despondent. The situation may look bad, but try to think positively. At least you are taking the first steps in controlling your time and, therefore, your life.

There are two ways to audit your time. Firstly, you could note how long you spend performing *each* task, without changing to something else. This means *everything*. For a few days, you need to note how long you spend making coffee, chatting about the football and even going to the loo. You need to include interruptions, checking your mail and making calls. In some cases, you may find that you spend only a few minutes on a task before becoming distracted. You will probably only be motivated to do this for a couple of days. However, it is a powerful way to underline just how uncontrolled your daily life is and how minor interruptions can have a profound impact.

The second approach uses a form divided into 15–30 minute sections. At the end of each hour, you write down how you spent the time. The problem with this method is that it fails to detect minor time thieves, such as interruptions that may take only two or three minutes but soon add up. It is often difficult to get going again once you have been interrupted, so such interruptions can be very disruptive.

Whichever approach you use, a time audit may offer some very sobering findings. It also helps you develop a sense of the value of time, especially if you cost it. Work out what you are worth each hour and minute of your working day either to yourself or your company. Then work out how much that talk about last night's TV programmes cost.

It is also worth performing a time audit if your main role is at home. How much time do you spend at the supermarket? How many times do you visit it each week? How much time do you spend at school coffee mornings? How much time do you spend on your hobbies? Note it all down. You should then be able to see why you cannot get a few minutes to yourself.

Enhance your productivity

Once you have performed your time audit, you can work towards enhancing your productivity. List the core tasks uncovered by your time audit (you may know these in advance). Then add up the time they currently take. You can also prioritise these according to the scale listed on page 93. This should allow you to see whether most of your time goes on the tasks that are both important and urgent.

Now set yourself a target time for each task. Try not to be over-ambitious – you do not want to sacrifice quality in the pursuit of speed. However, most of us can shave between 5 and 10 per cent off each task, especially by limiting the impact of the smaller time thieves (interruptions and so on).

Over the next couple of weeks, record how you are doing. Some tasks will prove impossible to perform more quickly. Others you will find you can do in much less time. For example, you may be able to save several hours by going to the supermarket once a week instead of daily. The only way you will know is to track your time.

You could also track the impact of each time and life management technique you introduce. In this case, the audit will highlight the small gains you have made and encourage you to keep going. You could, for example, complete a list, such as that suggested overleaf. You will need to complete the last column using a time audit. If you are trying to implement improved time and life management across a department, you will need to ask each member of staff to complete the form. Then compile the results into a master form.

The benefit offered by many changes may take several weeks to emerge. However, these gradual improvements mount up. It is a cliché – but true none the less – that Rome was not built in a day. Indeed, you need to expect setbacks and should allow yourself time to deal with them. However, this table is a way to confirm that you are making progress, which will encourage you continue. Psychologists call this 'positive reinforcement'. Now ask yourself: what have I done with that extra time? How does this fit with my mission statement? How does it take me closer to my goals at work and in life more generally?

Activity	New time and life management technique	Time saved
Reducing unnecessary phone calls		
Procrastination		
'To do' lists		
Email		
Reducing interruptions		
Managing meetings		

Work where and when you are most productive

In an ideal world, we would work where and when we are at our most productive. For example, more and more people work at home and find that their productivity increases. However, despite what some books and commentators would have you believe, this is not a universal experience.

A BT/*Management Today* survey (1998) of more than 400 managers revealed that just over half of them work from home at least part of the time and 30 per cent at least once a week. Of those who had experience of working from home, 48 per cent said that that was where they were most productive. On the other hand, 45 per cent said they were most productive in the office. Younger people and women seemed to benefit most from working at home: overall, 82 per cent of women, compared to 43 per cent of men, said they were more productive at home. Moreover, 66 per cent of under-35s said they were more productive at home. In other words, you need to discover where you work most productively and spend as much of your workday as you can in that environment.

As far as possible, you should also try to perform the most difficult tasks at the time in the day when you work most efficiently. Some of us tend to work best in the morning, others in the afternoon. There are good biological reasons underlying these variations. Many bodily functions – such as hormone production and, most obviously, sleep-wake cycles – vary throughout the day. Scientists call these patterns 'circadian variations'. Suffering from jet-lag underlines just how much of an impact throwing these rhythms out can have on our performance. To work out your 'performance circadian variation', track your energy and judge how alert you feel on a scale of one to ten every half-hour over a few days. Average out the scores and plot your performance over the day. Try to keep, if you can, the most physically and mentally demanding tasks for the times when your energy peaks and you are therefore at your most alert.

Planning is the key

Humans have always planned. Indeed, the ability to plan may be one feature that sets us apart from the rest of the animal kingdom. Our cave-dwelling ancestors planned how to hunt and farm. Today, planning is just as important. Taking the time to plan is, perhaps, the most effective way to impose order on the chaos that surrounds us. As a result, all time and life management relies on two key elements – a diary and a 'to do' list.

Use your diary

You probably already have a diary. Indeed, you may have several. However, it is better to use one diary for both your business and personal commitments. This avoids confusion and helps you keep a balance between your work, family and personal life. (It also means that you are less likely to forget birthdays and anniversaries.) Nevertheless, if you have a PA, ensure that he or she knows when you have arranged a meeting or have a personal commitment. This should reduce the number of conflicting bookings. If you use a paper-based system, try to write any appointments in pencil. This prevents your diary from looking like a Jackson Pollock painting or being caked in Tippex when meetings are cancelled or moved.

You can also use your diary to plan long-term projects. In some cases, this may not suffice and you may need to use sophisticated project-planning software, especially if you need to co-ordinate input of several people or companies. Nevertheless, in many cases a diary should suffice. For example, when the prolific Victorian novelist

Anthony Trollope started a book, he prepared a diary, divided into weeks for the time that he allowed himself. Each day he entered the number of pages he had written. As he noted: 'If at any time I have slipped into idleness for a day or two, the record of that idleness has been there, staring me in the face.'

If it is large enough, you can also use your diary to plan what you will do during the day and when. This may help you work in line with your performance rhythm. However, remember to build in some slack time for interruptions and unforeseen problems.

It is also worth using a year-to-view diary. You can mark on holidays, sales conferences and so on. You should set or agree your long-term deadlines in line with this view. As soon as you know which meetings you are expected to attend, mark your vacations.

Keep a 'to do' list

A 'to do' list is the second time and life management fundamental. Obviously, this lists your tasks along with any deadlines. Most time and life management books suggest that you should have a master list as well as a daily list, which you update each night. Advocates of this approach argue that the daily update helps clear your mind of any problems and stops you worrying overnight. Your 'to do' lists could also categorise tasks: writing, calls, emails and personal priorities. It is worth considering this if you need to perform a number of similar tasks – you tend to be more effective if you perform these in batches.

You should also break each large task down into smaller, more manageable pieces. This applies just as much to a major report analysing a market as it does to setting up a business or moving house. Try to define the task in a sentence. Then work out the broad stages that will allow you to reach the aim. For a report, for example, these stages might include: research, discussions, writing, revising and presentation. Then break each of these stages down into tasks. So, for the research stage, the tasks might include: visits to other companies; going to libraries; Internet searches; and so on. Then order these tasks in a logical progression and add these to your 'to do' list. The principle is one of 'divide and conquer' and, in this way, a large project suddenly becomes much less daunting. Depending on the overall time scale of the project, these tasks can then be interspersed with the rest of your work.

Once you have your master list, you need to establish your priorities. In some cases, this may mean simply picking the highest-priority job from the list and working your way down. You also need to prioritise your daily list. However, it is worth, if you can, interspacing dull tasks with interesting ones as well as alternating physical and mental tasks.

There are several ways in which you can prioritise your 'to do' list. The simplest is to list tasks in order of urgency. You can also mark each task from '1' (highest) to '10', or whatever is the least urgent. A more sophisticated approach considers whether each task is urgent, important, both or neither. Many people tend to tackle urgent jobs first, irrespective of their importance. As a result, they need to devote less quality time to their important tasks. So the quality of their work inevitably suffers. Assigning a value to each of these helps us to stop performing urgent or routine tasks simply out of habit.

Prioritising

Mark each task on your daily and master lists as follows::

A *important and urgent* You should do these tasks now.

B *important and less urgent* These are tasks that you need to do in the next couple of days, but at a time you are at your best, for example when your performance circadian variations peak (see page 91).

C *less important but urgent* These are tasks that you need to do in the next couple of days, but do not require you to be at your best. Much routine office administration falls into this category. You can also consider delegating C tasks (see page 137 for more advice on delegation).

D *less important and less urgent* You can do these tasks at your convenience. Again, consider delegation.

E *unimportant and not urgent* If it needs to be done some time, delegate. However, it might be better to bin it.

When you apply this lettering system the first few times, you will probably find that almost everything on your 'to do' list is either A or B. However, with practice you will find that you are better able to assess a task's priority accurately. Initially, you might find it worthwhile asking colleagues or your boss to help clarify the priority. On the other hand, if, after careful consideration, you still face a number of 'A' jobs, you have two choices. You could go for the shortest first; many people find that finishing a job gives them a psychological boost and the momentum carries over into other jobs on their list. Or you could tackle the most difficult and boring first – at least this way the dullest job is dispensed with. The choice is really up to you.

You need to keep your prioritisation up-to-date. In many cases, this may mean that you need to spend anything from 5 to 30 minutes each day rewriting the list, transferring the undone tasks to the next list, reassigning priorities and deciding how important and urgent new tasks are. The time you spend organising your workload pays itself back in improved effectiveness. However, if this takes up a considerable amount of time each day, consider investing in a personal information manager or palmtop computer (see below). Otherwise, it can feel rather like writing lines as a school punishment.

Whether you need to go high-tech depends on your job and lifestyle. Some people find a list that is updated weekly (ideally on a Friday night) suffices. You could use an A4 ring-bound notebook. This also allows you to jot down ideas, notes and phone calls in the book, keeping the record in one place. You can mark or highlight what you need to do today, and then cross out each task once it is done. However, ensure that you leave space for new tasks.

The daily or weekly review also allows you to examine how effective you have been. If you continually fail to reach your objectives, ask yourself:

- Am I trying to do much in too short a time?
- Could I have been better prepared?
- Did I assign the priorities correctly?
- Was there an unexpected interruption that threw my plans?
- Did I lack self-discipline?
- Were the tasks boring or too demanding?
- Did I procrastinate?
- Am I having problems with a particular person?

If a pattern emerges, see if there is anything you can do to improve the situation.

Take what is useful

While all time and life management depends, in one form or another, on a diary and a 'to do' list, you need to experiment and develop your system, rather than trying to shoe-horn your lifestyle into a prescribed system. What works for a business executive – who needs to juggle several meetings, phone calls and reports – may be inappropriate for an artist who needs to finish a large design over several weeks. So, it is important to discover what works for you and to decide which of the time and life management tips in the next three chapters can help you control your life.

Creative people often feel that living in chaos reflects their bohemian attitudes. But this misses the point. Even Karl Marx, who notoriously lived in a chaos of paper and notes, was able to find any item he needed quickly. And consider the advice of the French novelist Gustave Flaubert: 'Be regular and orderly in your life, so that you may be violent and original in your work.' Time and life management does not stifle creativity. Indeed, it liberates you from the problems that prevent you from doing the things at which you are best.

Nevertheless, many of the techniques advocated in time and life management books and courses simply do not work for everyone. Therefore, you may need to slaughter – or at least wound – a few of time and life management's sacred cows.

Firstly, for example, time and life management gurus often suggest blocking off time in your diary to devote yourself entirely to matters such as your A-list tasks or in order to work through your routine paperwork. They argue that *nothing* should impinge on this time: you should take your phone off the hook and ignore *all* interruptions. However, how many of us can do this? A doctor or nurse could hardly tell an ill patient to wait because now is their blocked-off time for routine paperwork. Or try telling a similar story to your boss. If you can block off time in this way, it is a great for focusing on the task in hand. However, try not to feel guilty if you cannot.

Secondly, many time and life management experts glibly suggest, 'Never handle a piece of paper more than once.' Certainly, piles of paper should not surround you. However, you will usually need to handle paper more than once. For example, while some time and life management books tell you to 'answer that letter and deal with the paper now', much correspondence may be only a C or D priority. If it is not urgent, it is fine to move correspondence into a pending file and think about it later.

The real point underlying the advice never to handle a piece of paper more than once is to make sure that you know where everything is, that you remain in control and that you avoid paper-shuffling. The advice also aims to reduce procrastination and to help you, where possible, to make immediate decisions. These are laudable aims, but do not take the advice literally.

Thirdly, many books suggest asking your assistant to highlight important aspects of a report or document. However, this relies on another person knowing what is important. With suggestions such as this, you need to be blunt and ask yourself why you are the manager. Presumably, it is because you are more experienced, knowledgeable and, therefore, more likely to know what really is important as well as better able to explore relationships and pick up synergies between items. As we will see in Chapter 7, creativity, increasingly a core management skill, depends on thinking beyond the conventional. Indeed, innovations often emerge at the junction between disciplines and theories and your experience and expertise is ever more likely to be the key factor that differentiates you from other people. The real message here is to keep the core tasks to yourself, but to delegate other jobs wherever possible. (Chapter 7 offers some advice on effective delegation.)

Finally, there is a current time and life management vogue for multitasking. This really means doing more than one thing at a time. Once again, this sacred cow is both a blessing and a curse. Certainly, we can use 'dead time' more effectively: we can read while on the exercise bike; we can listen to a business tape or learn a foreign language while in a car. But multitasking means that we tend to concentrate less and less on the task in hand. And that suggests that we could miss something important. In general, it is better to focus on the task before you.

The uses of modern technology

Perhaps it is a symptom of our time-pressured lives, but we can now choose from a multitude of paper-based and electronic time and life management systems. However, despite being quite dear, many of these can be complex to set up and end up being little more than an expensive 'to do' list, diary and address book.

Personal Information Managers

While some of us make do with a diary and a 'to do' list, other people find that a high-tech approach suits their lifestyle. Computer programs known as Personal Information Managers (PIMs) aim to offer faster access to information and perform routine time and life management tasks more rapidly. With a PIM, you should not need to keep scraps of paper and you can search your notes using keywords. Most PIMs offer a free text option that allows you to jot down notes. However, some allow you to include graphics and import financial information from spreadsheets. If you use a PIM, do not let these spiral into a virtual pile of paper: consider creating new sections – perhaps by project – and store information there.

Typically, for example, PIMs:

- automatically transfer unfinished 'to do' list items on to the next day's list
- warn of appointment clashes
- allow you to shift rapidly from a daily view to a weekly or yearly presentation. This helps you keep a long-term focus. For example, you can also use the yearly planner to allocate blocks of time for vacations, meetings, trade shows and so on
- require that you need to enter recurring events only once
- warn you about an event with an alarm
- link various parts of your electronic diary and time management organiser together as well as to other programs
- link notes or a spreadsheet to an event, such as a business meeting.

Most PIMs offer a number of other features, too:

- the contact file is useful if you have numerous contacts – accessing a particular number can be quicker than flicking through a box of cards or an address book. In some cases, the computer will even dial the number for you
- most PIMs allow you to log outgoing calls. For example, you can note the date and time of the call as well as recording the subjects discussed. This saves time if you need to track contacts for follow-up calls, budgets and contact reports

- you can log incoming calls either interfaced with the computer modem or free-standing. This helps you assess who calls you the most (this may help you discover the source of interruptions), which calls you need to follow up and which calls you should return
- PIMs allow you to print information out to fit your day planner
- some PIMs allow you to track time against projects, budgets, cost codes and so on. The code then appears under the appointment
- some PIMs allow you to create memos using name and address information from the contacts section
- the contacts section usually allows you to enter additional information – such as the assistant's name. Many have a free text option allowing you to add comments. Sales and PR people often use these to enter personal information – such as the names of the contacts' children
- in most cases, you can import and export the files into other databases, such as Lotus 1-2-3, Excel and FoxPro.

In practice, most PIMs available offer the same basic features: they allow you to track your appointments, calls, meetings and establish prioritised 'to do' lists. They also help you to record addresses, phone numbers and email addresses. After that, the choice is really down to you. Some PIMs come packaged with the software bundle on the PC. You can also choose from a range of programs, such as Lotus Organiser, Sidekick, and many more. You may wish to read some of the reviews or ask around for personal recommendations before investing in a PIM.

However, most of us use only a fraction of the facilities available to us on any computer program. So, take the time to read the manual as well as one of the additional books – such as the *10 Minute Guides* or *For Dummies* series. These offer tips that help you make the most of the program. Learning just one new technique a day – and this also applies to the word-processing, databases and other programs you use – can dramatically improve your effectiveness.

Networked PIMs

Some PIMs can now be installed on a network server, which makes possible group scheduling. Using some networked PIMs, you can access some or all of the group's calendars, allowing you to find a common time for a meeting. Many PIMs also offer centralised address books. In addition, if you are responsible for a project, you can manage the tasks of other group members and schedule meetings without having to track down each individual.

Similarly, web calendars (available at *www.yahoo.com* and *www.excite.com*) allow you to keep everyone in an amateur organisation in touch with the latest changes. These are free to societies and groups.

Palmtop organisers

In the 1980s, the personal organiser was the mark of being a business executive. In the 1990s, it was mobile phones and laptop computers. Today it is the palmtop computer that carries the kudos. Certainly, modern technology is now part of modern business life. A 1988 survey by BT and *Management Today* of 400 managers found that 78 per cent used mobile phones, 58 per cent laptop computers and 26 per cent computerised personal organisers. For some, these may be

---

Martin

As befits the Chief Executive of an innovative IT company, Martin Leuw of MediDesk is one senior manager well on his way to working in a paperless office. 'I went through my filing cabinet six months ago and realised that virtually nothing in the files was needed as it was all on the main server, but I'd carried on filing it anyway! When I joined MediDesk I decided virtually to stop using paper and bought a palmtop personal organiser. It has changed my life as well as accelerating my productivity and optimising my time and life management!'

Martin explains that the palmtop organiser carries all the essential information he needs. 'I no longer use paper for notes – it is all on my machine and easily retrievable. I compose emails, letters and presentations on the move from a tiny machine. All my contacts and appointments are available. My task list reminds me what to do and by when. It reminds me of birthdays, anniversaries etc.'

But what if Martin lost his palmtop? 'Everything is saved on my PC and I synchronise regularly,' he says. 'All in all it allows me to manage just a very hectic lifestyle and, from a time and life management viewpoint, raises my productivity significantly and reduces stress!'

'toys for the boys' (27 per cent of men had palmtop organisers, compared to 18 per cent of their female counterparts), but this belittles the value that palmtops offer some people, especially if they spend a lot of time away from the office.

So, how do you know if you need a PIM or palmtop? If you find problems keeping your 'to do' list up to date and if you need to reassign priorities regularly, a PIM or palmtop would probably help. A palmtop is better than a PIM if you are on the move. On the other hand, if you need to schedule regular meetings with your colleagues and to share a large number of contacts across the company, a network PIM may also prove a worthwhile investment.

Technological aids for disabled people

The Disability Discrimination Act 1995 aims to ensure that we are all treated equally at work and when applying for jobs. It obliges employers to make reasonable adjustments, such as providing specialist equipment where appropriate, to help employees carry out their tasks. Nevertheless, discrimination in the workplace is still rife. For example, whereas the unemployment figure for the general population is currently about 6 per cent, the figure within the deaf and hard-of-hearing population is around 15 per cent. And if you are deaf or hard-of-hearing and between the ages of 30 and 45, you are between six and nine times more likely to be unemployed than a non-disabled person.

Employers often cite problems with communication as one reason why they do not employ disabled people. However, modern technology offers many ways to communicate. It may also be able to transform your career prospects if you are disabled. For example, speech recognition can help people who cannot type.

One person in seven in the UK suffers from hearing loss, for example. However, buying a phone that is hearing-aid-compatible or using a portable amplifier can help you communicate if you have mild-to-moderate hearing loss. If you are more severely deaf, you can use a text phone (also called a minicom), which has a keyboard and a small display screen. You can then type messages, allowing direct communication with other text phones and contact with ordinary phones via the telephone relay service Typetalk. The Government's Access to Work programme will normally pay some or all of the cost of a text phone if you need one for work (they currently cost between £100 and £350, depending on the model, and a mobile text phone is also available). And although video telephones were originally developed to help people hold meetings in different places, they can also help you communicate if you use sign language.

At meetings, you could consider employing a speech-to-text operator. They can key in up to 200 words a minute, and the text is displayed on screen. Additionally, a printout can be made at the end of the meeting, which offers a useful record. Contact the Royal National Institute for Deaf People (RNID)★ for further information.

Similarly, there are technological advances that can help you work more effectively if you have impaired vision. Simple adjustments, such as altering the contrast on your computer screen and using text enlargement, may help you read off the screen more easily, but there are many other aids that can be of assistance. Web sites hosted by Microsoft★ and Apple★ offer further resources to enhance computer accessibility. These should help you optimise the computer for your needs, which should, in turn, enhance your time and life management.

For information and advice on technological help in the workplace, contact the Royal National Institute for the Blind,★ The Disability Alliance,★ RADAR★ or Ricability.★ If you are a student, you could also contact CanDo,★ a specialist careers information unit based at Lancaster University. For information on Access to Work contact your disability employment adviser or disability service team.

Be flexible

In our constantly changing world, whether you use a PIM or pen and paper, you need to remain flexible. Consider, for example, three common examples:

- if an unexpected problem upsets your carefully devised schedule, deal with the immediate problem and then re-evaluate your schedule
- if, as you progress towards your ultimate goal (see Chapter 4), you discover another core area that you need to consider, accept it and move forward with a revised plan
- relax some of your expectations in your relationships with your

spouse and children. Your kids probably know how you will react to a certain situation. Indeed, they may use this knowledge to provoke an argument or land the first strike. So relaxing your expectations defuses many problems before they arise. However, remember: being flexible is not the same as being a walkover.

Staying calm in a crisis

Judy Larkin, a founder of Regester Larkin, a London-based communications consultancy specialising in crisis management, emphasises the value of remaining in control and being flexible, as well as planning for a crisis. This should help you make the most of your resources in difficult times. And this applies just as much to your everyday life as to crises at work.

'In the same way as busy executives, preoccupied with the market pressures and financial performance needs of the current quarter, are not inclined to pay much attention to planning for possible crises, none of us wants to think about planning for major change, particularly if the outlook is unpleasant,' Judy says. 'However, Noah started building the ark *before* it began to rain!'

On the other hand, crises are often turning points in our lives at home and work. 'Virtually every crisis contains within itself the seeds of success as well as the roots of failure,' Judy comments. 'Finding, cultivating and harvesting the potential success is the essence of crisis management. Adverse or unpleasant events can, in fact, represent opportunities to build relationships, help establish a sense of competence and integrity and tackle difficult and important issues. Indeed, the Chinese definition of a crisis is represented by the words "threat" and "opportunity". Even in what may appear to be the darkest hour, constructive outcomes are possible and a renewed sense of purpose and momentum can be achieved.'

However, in any crisis – commercial or personal – time is at a premium and so effectively managing resources is critical. Henry Kissinger, the former US Secretary of State, once quipped: 'Next week there can't be any crisis. My schedule is already full!' Judy Larkin argues that this kind of time pressure means that following guidelines on actions to take and attitudes to adopt under pressure is essential. Against this background, she suggests that successful crisis management in a fast-moving world involves:

- recognising you have a crisis
- taking the appropriate actions to remedy the situation
- being *seen* to take them
- being *heard* to say the right things.

'In the commercial world, companies often misclassify a problem by focusing on the technical aspects of what's happened and ignoring issues of perception,' Judy says. 'Recent corporate history is strewn with examples: Pan Am's failure to communicate in the aftermath of the Lockerbie tragedy in 1989; P&O's commitment of a cardinal sin at the time of the Zebrugge ferry disaster by speculating that the ferry hit the harbour walls; Shell's ineffective response to Greenpeace over the disposal of the Brent Spar; and, of course, the British government's abysmal performance over BSE.

'When a tanker spills millions of gallons of oil into the sea, or an aeroplane falls out of the sky, or a ferry turns turtle in the water, people's first reaction is one of shock. It is difficult to accept that such disasters can still occur in this age of advanced technology and environmental consciousness,' Judy remarks. 'Ultimately, no one expects to live in a risk-free world. Accidents happen in our private lives and in business. This initial sense of shock, however, quickly turns to anger if an organisation or individual at the centre of the crisis is not seen to take the appropriate action and to say the appropriate words.'

Against this background, Judy notes that in any crisis, personal or corporate, we want to know:

- what happened?
- why?
- whose fault was it?
- when did persons concerned first think it might happen?
- what are they doing now?
- how can we be sure that it will not happen again?

But, most importantly, she suggests that we want to know: 'Why should we trust you?'

Meanwhile, Judy adds that people at the centre of the crisis will feel the pressure build. They will sense surprise; find that they lack information; face an escalating flow of events; and endure the feeling that they have lost control. They will also be under intense scrutiny, leading to a siege mentality and panic. Nevertheless, people need to be quickly reassured about certain things, essentially that:

- everything – it is hoped – was in place to try to prevent the crisis from happening in the first place
- as soon as the crisis occurred, those responsible had plans and resources in place to resolve the situation as quickly as possible – painting a picture of a group of competent, caring people, swinging into action really quickly to handle events as they unfolded.

'But above everything else,' Judy says, we want to know that 'those involved really cared about what happened.

'Following the British Midland Kegworth aeroplane crash in 1989, the airline's chairman, Sir Michael Bishop, immediately raced to the scene of the accident giving live radio interviews from his car phone,' Judy says. 'His response was remarkable. Many people in senior management positions are fearful of being misreported by the media and will not give interviews until they have all the facts. In a crisis situation, this can be disastrous because it takes too long, and communication has to begin immediately. Sir Michael gave interviews when he had no knowledge about the cause of the accident, how many people had been involved and so on. Faced with this dilemma, he focused on expressing how he felt about what had happened and what he was going to do about the situation. This helped to reassure people that British Midland would do whatever was necessary to look after those involved, would leave no stone unturned to find out the cause of the crash and, above all, cared deeply.

'Taking action in a crisis can be fraught with risk,' Judy adds. 'A strategy is needed for deciding when to define a situation as a crisis, when to take action and when to work with others in solving the crisis. Such an organised and strategic sense is in itself a great advantage when tensions develop. The ability to keep cool when everything is collapsing is a quality valued in leaders, especially since apparent confidence shown by the leader is so reassuring to colleagues.'

Judy argues that planning for a personal or business crisis makes it more possible to concentrate on the problem when it peaks and provides a framework for action. 'Crisis management is about seizing the initiative – taking control of what has happened before it engulfs the organisation or individuals involved,' she says. 'Good time management, adopting a checklist mentality, is absolutely critical under pressure in order that commitments can be properly structured, resources and time carefully rationed, and those involved can respond to unfolding events in a practical, responsible and sensitive manner.'

So, Judy suggests the following:

- develop a positive attitude towards crisis management
- understand the risk and acknowledge what has happened
- consider ways to improve processes and performance (for example, through improved health and safety standards, staff training and so on)
- put in place early warning systems to monitor potential problems
- establish a clear process for communication
- know who needs to be communicated with and talk in ways that relate to concern and emotion
- work with third parties to establish credibility
- focus on building trust as well as good information.

'And remember,' she concludes, 'progress is better than perfection.'

Learn to simplify

In a sense, the aim of time and life management can be summed up in a single word: *simplify*. The techniques discussed in the next chapters aim to make life simpler at home and at work. For example, several suggestions ask you to question whether you really need to perform some routine tasks.

However, at the same time, trying to simplify your life means being proactive: getting rid of clutter (see Chapter 8); controlling your personal finances (see Chapter 9); and tackling time and life management at home and work (see Chapters 7 and 9). All this should mean that life in general becomes more straightforward, and that should free your time for other things.

Learning to 'just say no'

Agreeing to an unreasonable demand from a boss, partner or child is probably one of the leading time-wasters. How many hours and weeks do you waste simply because you do not say no when you have the chance? No doubt you say yes to please someone. But who are you trying to please? And how effective will you be if you are doing something that you do not really want to do?

You have to learn to say no to any demand that you feel is unreasonable, either because you do not have sufficient time or because the demand does not fit with your personal ethical view. You may even gain respect for knowing when to say no. After all, it is far worse to agree to a request and then to back out, which inevitably means letting down a colleague or friend.

Therefore, before agreeing, ensure that you know what you are letting yourself in for. Some tasks can be more time-consuming than they appear. (Once again, add between 10 and 25 per cent to any time estimate.) You could also put a time limit on your commitment – say that you will be able to help for a couple of hours a week, for example – and stick to it. Understanding your core values (see page 69) makes it easier to say no without feeling guilty.

If your boss makes the unreasonable demand, remind him or her of your other high-priority tasks, and ask which need to be sacrificed. Do not feel guilty about this – deciding between competing high-priority tasks is a key management skill. If you are the manager, try to decide which aspects of the work you need to perform and which you can delegate or reassign among your staff. It is also worth helping out your boss. Explain, for example, that you cannot work on a particular project immediately but will be able to the following week. This can be difficult to broach, but it will become easier with practice.

Develop your negotiating capacity

Learning to say no is one reason why developing your negotiating capacity is a key strategy to help you cope and progress in whatever circumstances you find yourself. However, this means understanding how we interact when we communicate. In the 1950s and '60s, the American psychologist Eric Berne suggested looking at the way we communicate as three behavioural modes: *parent*, *adult* or *child*. Understanding these modes can help your develop your negotiating skills and tailor your strategy to particular situations. If you are aware of your behaviour, you are better placed to do something about it, in part by using the time and life management techniques.

In the *parent mode*, you are either critical or nurturing. You may tell your subordinates at work, for example, that they *must* do something. This is the *oppressive parent* mode. However, you can also show your caring side. If a member of staff has a problem, for example, you may show this caring side by offering to 'look after it for them'. This is the *supportive parent* mode.

The *adult mode* is most obvious when you are speaking to your peers or your spouse. In this mode, you take rational, balanced decisions, free of prejudices, obligations or emotions. On the other hand, the *child mode* (which is also known as the *infant mode*) lets your emotions run away with you. You move into this mode when you experience happiness, anger, jealousy or fear. The child mode also includes curiosity.

We can be in more than one mode at a time. For example, when giving a presentation to peers, you may be in the adult or parent mode. The presentation itself may be a parent transaction, while the discussion afterwards is in the adult mode. However, you may also have something of the child in you because of nerves, anxiety and so on. When faced with your boss, you may also be in the child mode, while you are more likely to talk to a peer 'parent-to-parent' – if discussing the unsatisfactory performance of an employee, for example, with the human resource manager. Finally, there is the 'child-to-child' interaction, when you joke around with a friend.

Problems can arise from crossed transactions. This might happen when you receive an answer that you do not expect or when you respond in a way that is not expected by the person with whom you are communicating. A peer may want an adult-to-adult or even an adult-to-supportive-parent conversation about a problem at work. However, if you answer by discussing your problems, you are in the child mode.

Other problems arise when people become stuck in a dominant state. People stuck in the dominating or supportive parent state are authoritarian. At best, they are benign – many doctors are stuck in the supportive parent mode. At worse, they are bullies, and people stuck in the adult mode tend to be cold and calculating. At the other extreme, people stuck in the child mode are often unable to make decisions.

Nevertheless, you can manipulate these transactions. Marriage guidance counsellors often use transactional analysis with their clients. You can also use transactional analysis to help understand and motivate your staff and work colleagues. It can be particularly helpful when you face the difficult task of criticising others.

Thinking in these terms can help you tailor the conversation to the person. One member of your staff – perhaps someone who is immature or young – may respond best to a supportive parent approach. Another may respond best to an adult-to-adult interaction, especially if they are more mature. For example, as a boss, you can move from parent to adult mode – and encourage an employee to move from child to adult mode – by putting a question in a particular manner. For example, this might be by stating, first of all, 'We know what is wrong,' and then suggesting, 'These are the options,' before asking, 'Which do you favour?'.

Transactional analysis can also help you understand your responses. If you feel humiliated and clench your fists during a difficult telephone conversation, you may be in the child mode. If you always procrastinate, you may also favour the child mode. Developing decision-making strategies can help bolster your adult mode. However, the aim is to keep lines of communication open and avoid confrontations, not to dominate and manipulate other people.

Overcoming shyness

Many people agree to unreasonable demands because they lack the self-confidence to tackle difficult situations. In other words, they feel shy. A few people suffer from social phobia: a psychiatric disorder characterised by intense, irrational and persistent fear of scrutiny by other people. The sufferer fears humiliation or embarrassment. Studies suggest that around 8 per cent of the population during any year and around 14 per cent during their lifetime suffers from social phobia, making it the most common psychiatric disorder after substance abuse and depression.

Social phobia can be debilitating– and it is far more serious than the nerves that most people feel when they have to make a presentation or appear on stage. Certainly, people with social phobia are unable to speak or perform in public. But they may also be unable to write a cheque, use the phone or eat when they are being watched. To minimise the intense anxiety that they feel in the presence of other people, social phobia sufferers often avoid likely trigger situations. Inevitably, their work and social life suffers.

Social phobia undermines career progression. Sufferers may be unable to cope with driving tests and oral examinations. Indeed, around 16 per cent of social phobia patients are estimated to be unemployed, compared to about 6 per cent in the healthy population. Moreover, 70 per cent develop other psychological problems: almost half become agoraphobic, for example; almost a fifth abuse alcohol; while almost as many experience major depression.

Fortunately, a combination of psychological approaches and drugs usually alleviates social phobia. So, for example, learning relaxation techniques (see page 127), training in social skills and gradual exposure to the fear situation can all help people suffering from social phobia face difficult situations. A number of drugs can support these psychological approaches. Contact your GP if you feel that you may suffer from social phobia.

However, shyness is far more common. The psychologist Bernardo Carducci suggests that almost half the population are shy. In addition, it seems to be a growing problem – or at least one of which we are now more aware. Indeed, over the last 15 years, the proportion of people who regard themselves as shy rose from 40 to 48 per cent. Of these, 62 per cent feel shy every day. Meeting strangers and the opposite sex are the two major triggers. In 1995, *Psychology Today* asked readers to answer a survey about shyness. It found that shy people often need more time to 'warm up' to a new situation – including meetings and social events – and tend to make unfair comparisons with other people. So, a shy person tends to compare him- or herself to the life and soul of the party. Inevitably, this only exacerbates their shyness.

So, what is the answer? Dr Carducci suggests not regarding shyness as something *within* you. 'Stop dwelling on your own insecurities and become more aware of the people around you,' he suggests. That might mean scheduling time for your social life – which is something naturally gregarious people already do. This increases your opportunities to practise your social skills.

However, that does not always mean scheduling time for the pub. Dr Carducci advises volunteering, which moves your focus from inside you to other people. It may mean – if you find opening a conversation difficult or fear the periodic silences when talking with someone –

rehearsing some lines to begin a conversation and working on ways to keep a conversation going. Moreover, think positively – if you expect a negative response, you will probably get one. Be interested in other people. It is also worth remembering that there is a 50:50 chance that the person you are speaking to is at least as shy as you.

Tricks to help boost your self-esteem

There are a number of tricks you can try to boost your self-esteem, many of which work on the principle that transforming yourself on the outside leads to an internal change. Other methods aim to improve your view of yourself. If your life script (Chapter 3) means that you tend to hold yourself in poor esteem, it will emerge in everything you do. And that could hold you back. You will be less able to say no to unreasonable demands and you will be less likely to push forward towards your ultimate life goals. In other words, a lack of self-esteem can undermine your best attempts at time and life management. So, you could try some of the following tricks to boost your self-esteem.

(1) Visualise yourself succeeding and mentally push away negative thoughts.

(2) Do not compare yourself to other people, either favourably or unfavourably. If you compare your self unfavourably, you will obviously lower your self-esteem. And if you compare yourself favourably with others, they may exceed your expectations, which will undermine your judgement and further lower your self-esteem.

(3) Volunteer for charity work. Volunteering reduces the feeling of isolation and self-absorption.

(4) Avoid people who run you down, meddle in your affairs or stab others in the back – if they do this to others, the chances are that they are probably doing it to you too.

(5) Look after your appearance. Having a haircut or buying new clothes tends to boost self-esteem.

(6) Do not take yourself too seriously – keep smiling. This means that the people around you are more likely to smile with you and respond positively.

(7) Think about the non-verbal cues that you give out. Psychologists

believe that some 80 per cent of any message we give out or receive is non-verbal. Only 20 per cent comes from the words we use or hear. If you have a downcast look and slumped shoulders, people will tend to believe that you are depressed and lacking in confidence and commitment, no matter what you say or how you feel. And, of course, the converse is equally true.

(8) Consider assertiveness training. If you have problems being assertive when you need to be, assertiveness training can help you stand up for your rights, without infringing anyone else's. During assertiveness training you might, for instance, act out situations where you need to say no – such as to refuse an unreasonable request to work late. The trainer can then comment on your performance (which is sometimes videotaped), focusing on elements such as your vocal style and body language – remember, most of the message you send is non-verbal. It can be a sobering experience, but assertiveness training is a very effective way to boost your self-esteem. Many adult education centres run assertiveness training courses. Contact your local library or adult education centre for details.

Counselling

If all this fails, consider counselling. Counselling, which essentially aims to help people regain control of their lives, can be as effective as drugs for relatively minor psychiatric conditions, such as some cases of anxiety, milder depression (especially when linked to life events such as grief or the menopause) and obsessions. Moreover, work-based counselling can help resolve issues such as lack of effective communication and consultation, lack of job security and irregular hours.

Indeed, with the continuing erosion of family and community support structures, many people still need someone to talk to. The Samaritans receives more than four million calls a year – about one every nine seconds – and the number of calls increased by 30 per cent between the mid-1980s and mid-'90s. Counselling seems to work best when you suffer from a defined problem. Counsellors can offer a refreshing new perspective on a problem that is undermining your self-esteem or which forms an important strand in your life script. In other words, counselling can give your attempts at time and life management a much-needed boost.

There are more than 11,000 counsellors currently practising in the UK. This means that almost everyone will be able to find someone they can talk to easily. Remember that the relationship between a client and counsellor can be intimate: trust is essential when you are airing your hopes, fears and anxieties.

Many GPs either employ or have close links to a local counsellor. You can drop in to your practice and ask at reception whether they can recommend someone. The British Association of Counselling★ can also put you in touch with counsellors in your area. Next, interview the counsellor. Most counsellors hold an initial consultation to ask you about your problems and background. You can use this initial consultation to ensure that you are happy exposing your thoughts and feelings to this person. Ask about the counsellor's experience, qualifications and even interests beyond work; obtain references if you wish. However, counselling is also about empathy, and so it is important that you feel comfortable in the counsellor's company.

Psychotherapy

If you want to explore fully why your life script is undermining your self-esteem you could consider psychotherapy, which examines the unconscious causes of your problems and emotions. Psychotherapists aim to enhance your sense of wellbeing and alleviate stress and anxiety. A vast choice of approaches is available – some 250 schools offer variations on a range of themes.

Some help you gain an insight into your past and present relationships by exploring your subconscious. Others offer practical help for specific problems, without exploring the subconscious. Many analysts integrate a number of techniques that seem to be the most effective for a particular problem. However, a therapist's relationship with a client is probably more important than the theoretical underpinning.

Your attitudes are just as important. Psychotherapy is hard work. You need to want to change and believe that the therapy will help. In many cases, you will need to make a considerable investment of time and money. So, ensure that you are compatible with the therapy. It is also worth looking back on the stage of change model introduced in Chapter 3.

The various approaches therapists can take (explored in detail in *The Which? Guide to Managing Stress*) fall broadly into two groups: *psychoanalysis* and *cognitive behavioural therapy*.

Psychoanalysts believe that the roots of our psychological illness lie buried in our unconscious. Often these roots are so deeply buried that we are unaware of the cause of a particular distress. Psychoanalysis exposes the roots, which helps the patient understand his or her problems, subconscious motivations and repressed desires. As a result, psychoanalysis is often a long, difficult and sometimes even painful experience.

The other main approach, cognitive behavioural therapy, aims to replace unhelpful coping strategies with behaviour and attitudes that are more appropriate, without necessarily gaining an insight into the causes. These therapists begin by analysing your unhelpful coping strategies. This reveals the behaviour that you need to change in order to boost your self-esteem, for example, and overcome obsessive, addictive behaviour patterns, which waste time and can prove self-destructive. The analysis also uncovers the conditions that trigger, maintain and exacerbate the unhelpful coping strategies. Using a mixture of several techniques, the therapist then encourages positive behaviour and replaces a destructive thought pattern with a more realistic, positive and enjoyable approach to life.

Behavioural approaches tend work more rapidly than psychoanalysis if you suffer from a specific problem. Indeed, behavioural approaches are widely used by psychiatrists to help people suffering from post-traumatic stress disorder, phobias, anxiety, and so on. However, different therapies suit different people. For example, psychotherapy helps people who are unable to adjust to change, who are articulate, able to see the roots of their problems and able to cope with delving into painful areas. Behavioural approaches are more appropriate when there is a specific phobia or social skill problem, such as aggression or lack of assertiveness.

As a result, behavioural approaches may be effective if you are unable to say no to unreasonable demands. Psychoanalysis may be more appropriate if you want to understand why you wrote your life script in the way you did. But both approaches aim to help you take responsibility for your behaviour by changing attitudes, ideas and expectations. And both should help you along the road to effective time and life management.

The British Confederation of Psychotherapists* publishes a register of over 1,200 qualified therapists from a number of organisations. They also offer advice on how to find a therapist. You can also be referred on the NHS.

Ten basic principles of time and life management

Time and life management can be reduced to ten basic principles. These principles offer you a supportive structure while you examine your life, implement new ways of working and move towards your ultimate ambition.

(1) Develop a personal philosophy and value set.

(2) Understand where you want your life to go. Identify long-term goals that are in line with your philosophy and value set and that take you towards your ultimate destination in life.

(3) Then identify short-term goals that are in line with this philosophy and value set and that help you reach each long-term goal.

(4) Balance your work, family and personal commitments. Again, this should be in line with your personal philosophy and value set. So, learn to say no.

(5) Plan each day, using a diary and 'to do' list.

(6) Spend 80 per cent of your time at home and at work on your priorities.

(7) Organise and simplify your life at home and at work.

(8) Manage your health as carefully as you manage your work (see next chapter).

(9) Be committed to life-long learning. However, take what is useful and question any advice you are given to see what is appropriate for you. In time and life management, there are no sacred cows.

(10) Audit your progress at all levels, from the impact of small changes to the progress you are making towards your ultimate destination in life.

Chapter 6

Increase your time

Fundamentally, time and life management aims to help you perform more effectively and efficiently – at home, at work and at play. You would not expect peak performance from a 10-year-old computer running the most up-to-date software. Nor would you expect to draw a detailed technical diagram with a blunt pencil. Yet we expect to perform at our best when we are tired and fatigued, when we have not eaten a healthy diet, and when we have not relaxed physically or mentally for weeks.

Of course, you cannot increase time. However, looking after yourself means that you will feel less fatigued, you will work more effectively and achieve more in the time available. Indeed, you may even be able to get up earlier in the mornings, an ideal way to gain more time, while avoiding fatigue – one of the leading reasons underlying poor performance, as well as one of the worst enemies of effective time and life management. If you feel tired and sleepy, you are less likely to feel motivated – or even have the energy – to implement the changes you identified earlier in the book. This chapter examines some ways in which you can reduce fatigue and bolster your performance, thereby enhancing your time and life management.

Fatigue – a common problem

Fatigue is almost as common as poor time and life management.

In one survey of patients consulting their GPs, the results of which were published in 1999 in *Psychological Medicine*, researchers found that between 13 and 15 per cent suffered from 'pure' fatigue. (In other words, the fatigue was not caused by another physical or psychological condition). Around a fifth of these had suffered from fatigue for at least six months. This suggests that one person in six in a GP's waiting room suffers from 'pure' fatigue. Remember that these are the people who decide the problem is severe enough to consult their GP.

Fatigue risk factors

A number of factors seem to increase the risk of suffering from fatigue, including insomnia, 'sick building syndrome' (see below) and certain prescription drugs. For example, a study published in 1999 in *Medical Care* suggests that women tend to report suffering from fatigue more frequently than men. On the other hand, among younger and more highly educated people, both men and women are more likely to complain of fatigue than their older, less well-educated counterparts. This group was also more likely to suffer from physical and psychosocial problems and felt less well overall. Factors specific to women, such as the menopause and periods, contributed to fatigue (excessive bleeding can cause anaemia, which contributes to tiredness, for example), as did caring for young children while being employed.In contrast, being disabled or suffering from a serious illness were the main reasons underlying fatigue among men.

However, this study depended on patients' willingness to respond to a questionnaire. Women might be more willing to *admit* to suffering from fatigue, whereas men traditionally try to 'tough it out'.

Moreover, both daytime sleepiness and fatigue become more common as we get older. Finnish researchers, for example, found in 1998 that one middle-aged person in ten suffers from daytime sleepiness. Reporting their results in the *European Journal of Neurology*, they found, not surprisingly, that shift-workers and those working irregular hours were especially vulnerable. However, apart from being dangerous, daytime sleepiness and fatigue compromise your ability to work and live productively. In many ways, fatigue is the worst enemy of time and life management.

Furthermore, a number of commonly used medicines increase the likelihood of feeling sleepy and fatigued, including some beta-blockers (used to lower blood pressure), some anti-anxiety drugs and antidepressants, and, predictably, sleeping tablets. Despite the well-publicised dangers of over-using sleeping pills – which include impaired mental performance the next day and slowed reaction times – some 12 per cent of elderly people take hypnotics every night. In nursing homes, this increases to a third. If you take sleeping pills (such as benzodiazepines), try some of the sleep hygiene techniques outlined below. Many people find they work at least as well.

Do not stop taking benzodiazepines abruptly: this can lead to a potentially serious withdrawal syndrome. (Benzodiazepines are sometimes called tranquillisers, anxiolytics or hypnotics. Some other drugs also come into these categories. If in doubt, ask your doctor or pharmacist.) First, speak to your doctor, who can help you gradually reduce your dose.

Moreover, some benzodiazepines – including nitrazepam, flunitrazepam and flurazepam – tend to have a longer duration of action than others, such as loprazolam, lormetazepam and temazepam. The latter benzodiazepines may be less likely to undermine your performance the next day. However, they are more likely than the longer-acting drugs to cause withdrawal reactions if you stop taking them suddenly.

Some other medications are perhaps more surprising causes of daytime fatigue and impaired performance. For instance, beta-blockers – such as propranolol, atenolol and carvedilol – are highly effective for lowering blood pressure, but can cause fatigue and sleep disturbances. Another group of blood pressure-lowering drugs, called the ACE inhibitors (these include captopril, enalapril and lisinopril), can lead to a persistent dry cough, which can also cause fatigue. Many other classes of drugs also lower blood pressure. So, if you believe that your fatigue worsened since you started taking beta-blockers, consult your doctor.

Similarly, some antihistamines – used to treat hayfever and some other allergic conditions – may cause daytime sleepiness and even impair driving ability. Certainly, poorly controlled hayfever can lead to poor-quality sleep and, therefore, daytime fatigue, as well as undermining performance at school and work and ruining quality of life for several months each year. However, the choice of treatment is important if you are to avoid further undermining your performance. Ask your doctor or pharmacist for an antihistamine that is less likely to cause drowsiness.

Getting a good night's sleep

We have been searching for millennia for ways to get a good night's sleep and counter fatigue. The Ancient Egyptians drank wine and used opium to help them sleep. Western herbalists used a number of plants – including hops, skullcap and valerian – that form part of herbal remedies today. Then, during the 1960s, drug companies launched the benzodiazepines, which we now know are highly addictive and can undermine your performance the next day.

Despite this, insomnia remains common. A 1994 survey of 195 insomniacs who called a nurse-run help-line run by the charity Medical Advisory Service underlined this. The results do not reveal the ages, but three-quarters said their lack of sleep made them moody or depressed. A third reported problems with family and friends and 62 per cent said that lack of sleep undermined concentration. This is hardly a recipe for effective time management.

Moreover, the telephone survey highlighted the fact that the misery of insomnia can last for years. Almost one in five of those interviewed said that they had suffered with insomnia for more than a decade, while 8 per cent endured sleepless nights for more than 20 years. On average, men suffered from insomnia for five years, compared to 7.5 years among women.

Other studies confirm that insomnia exerts a heavy psychological toll from sufferers. Apart from making you feel miserable, chronic insomnia increases the likelihood that the sufferer will develop depression around 14-fold, the likelihood of suffering from anxiety 25-fold and abusing alcohol threefold. Indeed, insomnia and poor-quality sleep undermine our daytime performance, with the result that we need to work harder and harder to keep pace. Therefore, we are less able to get a good night's sleep. So we are more likely to feel fatigued. In other words, it is easy to become trapped in a cycle of fatigue and insomnia.

A good night's sleep is central to being alert during the day. It will enhance your performance and help you implement the time and life management strategies outlined in this book. Indeed, if you get a good night's sleep you may be able to get up earlier in the morning. In addition, while sleep problems are common, most people can overcome insomnia without using tablets, by following these simple rules:

- **treat any underlying disease** Arthritis pain, depression – because it can cause early morning waking – and sleep apnoea (whereby people snore more and more loudly then jerk awake as they appear to stop breathing) can make getting a good night's sleep difficult for individuals and their partners

- **avoid nicotine, caffeine and alcohol**, especially just before bed. Caffeine means you will go to bed later, wake earlier and sleep less well. An alcoholic nightcap may help you fall asleep. However, as blood alcohol levels fall, sleep becomes lighter and more fragmented. Alcohol also exacerbates sleep apnoea, while nicotine can act as a stimulant

- **go to bed only when tired or sleepy** but keep regular bedtimes (so do not go to bed early one night if you are a bit sleepy)

- **do not count sheep** If you cannot get to sleep, get up and do something

- **get up at the same time**, even on weekends and holidays. Try not to spend more than eight hours in bed. Most people only need between 6 and 8 hours sleep. So work out your average sleep requirement and aim to achieve that

- **exercise regularly in the morning, late afternoon or early evening** Exercising in outdoor sunlight may be especially beneficial. (Sunlight helps set the sleep-wake cycle.) Note, however, that exercising just before bedtime can make sleep more difficult

- **use the bedroom only for sleep and sex** Do not read, watch television, eat etc. in bed. You want to create an association between the bedroom and sleep. Some people fall asleep on the sofa in front of *Newsnight*, for example, but are then wide awake when they go to bed. In this case, they associate the bedroom with not sleeping

- **avoid daytime naps** You need only a certain amount of sleep each 24 hours. Therefore, if you sleep during the day, you will need less sleep at night

- **do not eat just before bed** – especially if you find spicy meals upset your stomach. If you are hungry, eat a light snack.

- **limit your fluid intake** in the couple of hours before bed if you find that nocturnal visits to the bathroom disrupt your sleep

- **do not brood in bed** Anxiety is a leading cause of insomnia. In some cases, this may be severe enough to need medical attention (talk to your GP). In minor cases, or if you are tormented by day-to-day cares, write down your worries before you go to bed and place the list where you will not be tempted to examine it until the next morning

- **use relaxation techniques** (see below) and breathing techniques. Take some time out to unwind before going to bed. You could read (but not in bed), take a bath or listen to soothing music
- **entice yourself to bed** Make the bed as comfortable as possible and make the bedroom a relaxing, welcoming place.
- **establish a routine** Remember how you got your kids to bed – or how your parents got you to sleep? You probably followed a bedtime routine – a bath followed by bedtime story perhaps. So take your own advice and establish a regular routine: check that the house is locked up, brush your teeth and set the alarms, for example.

Together, these sleep hygiene techniques are often enough to help you get a good night's rest, avoid daytime fatigue and help you operate at your peak performance without resorting to drugs.

The Royal College of Psychiatrists★ produces a patient information leaflet and Talking Life★ offers audio tapes that address sleep problems.

Jet lag

Today more and more people travel across numerous time zones for business or pleasure. However, jet lag often undermines their performance once they arrive at their destination. Fortunately, you can take a number of steps to beat jet lag:

- avoid stimulants during the flight, including coffee, tea and cola
- avoid alcohol before and during the flight. Alcohol promotes dehydration, and dehydration is a common cause of poor performance and fatigue (see below). This can exacerbate the effects of jet lag
- try to keep going: sleep as little as possible until the night after landing or until the local bedtime
- if all else fails, consider a short course of sleeping pills to help establish a local sleeping pattern. However, you should avoid using sleeping tablets for more than a few days, and heed the warnings on page 116.

Toxic overload, fatigue and 'sick building syndrome'

Despite our growing awareness of green issues, each day we face a heavy chemical bombardment. The days of the great London smog of 1952, which lasted five days and killed 4,000 people through associated illnesses, may be gone. (A cross-party alliance of MPs and public health doctors formulated the Clean Air Act of 1956. Emissions fell by 65 per cent between 1954 and 1979.) However, we are still exposed to industrial chemicals, pesticides, food additives and heavy metals, as well as legal and illegal drugs. Even the buildings in which we work and live may reduce immunity and contribute to fatigue.

For example, lead poisoning can cause fatigue and a variety of other unpleasant symptoms. In the early part of the twentieth century children became ill after sucking on cribs decorated with lead-containing paints. More recently, people have been poisoned by lead from car emissions and leached from water pipes. Long-term exposure to even low levels of lead can cause depression and confusion, as well as learning and behavioural difficulties.

More and more people are now doing up old houses. If you are one of them, get rid of any pipes made of lead. These are far less common than they were, but remain in a few older houses. In 1996, researchers from Glasgow University reported in the *British Medical Journal* that 17 per cent of houses in one area had levels of lead in their water above the widely accepted safe level. (However, this was down from almost half in 1981.) If you are in doubt, ask your water provider for information. Making formula feeds with tap water in houses with lead pipes can expose babies to dangerous levels. In the Glasgow study, 13 per cent of bottle-fed babies were exposed to dangerous lead levels. Old paint may be a more common source of lead. Many people used simply to paint or paper over old paint. Stripping paper and paint can release lead-laden dust. So do not let children eat paint chips or play on floors covered with old paint dust.

'Sick building syndrome'

Against this background, there is a growing recognition that sick building syndrome commonly causes fatigue and other conditions. The World Health Organisation recognises sick building syndrome as a disease characterised by dry or itchy skin and irritation of the

121

respiratory-digestive tracts and the eyes, combined with headaches, nausea and fatigue.

The problem seems to lie in modern ventilation systems. In two studies published in 1996 (in *Epidemiology* and *Occupational and Environmental Medicine*), workers in mechanically ventilated and air-conditioned environments were six times more likely to suffer sick building syndrome than those in naturally ventilated buildings. Therefore, the answer seems to be to get some fresh air into the office. Improving ventilation reduced the 'sick building' symptoms, such as fatigue.

The sick house syndrome

Your house may also be contributing to your sense of malaise and fatigue. In 1999, Finnish researchers released results of a study of the health of people living in 310 houses, 52 per cent of which had a moisture problem and 27 per cent of which showed signs of mould. According to these, published in the *European Respiratory Journal*, people living in damp housing were more likely to suffer sinusitis and acute bronchitis, as well as nocturnal cough and breathlessness, than those living in the drier houses. Breathlessness can undermine sleep quality and leave you fatigued the next day – a common problem among people with asthma (see *The Which? Guide to Managing Asthma*). People in damp housing are also more likely to suffer sore throats, the common cold and tonsillitis.

Similarly, people living in houses with mould are more likely to contract a cold, cough during the day and at night, and suffer from sore throats and rhinitis. Moreover, mould exposure produces fatigue and difficulty concentrating. Obviously, these factors undermine performance and limit your ability to manage your time and life.

Drink enough water

Most of us could benefit from drinking more water each day. Simple as it sounds, drinking water could improve productivity and reduce fatigue. According to a review of the scientific evidence published in the *Journal of the American Dietetic Association* in 1999, the average sedentary adult man needs at least 2,900ml of fluid a day, while the average sedentary adult woman needs at least 2,200ml. This does not necessarily mean water – you can also get fluid through noncaffeinated, non-alcoholic beverages, soups and foods. Indeed, solid foods contribute around 1,000ml of fluid each day. Nevertheless, a man needs almost 2 litres and a woman 1.5 litres of noncaffeinated, non-alcoholic fluid a day.

As a result of not getting sufficient fluid, many people are chronically mildly dehydrated. Just 2 per cent dehydration can impair several aspects of physical and psychological performance, including contributing to fatigue. Indeed, fatigue is often the first sign of dehydration. More seriously, low fluid consumption contributes to a number of conditions including urinary stones, obesity and even certain cancers. Several factors increase the likelihood of dehydration, such as finding water 'boring', drinking diuretics, such as caffeine and alcohol, exercise and warm days.

But you do need to drink water – and plenty of it. Drink at least six glasses of water every day – more if you exercise regularly. Drinking water is a simple way to help you perform at your peak.

Coffee – only a short-term boost

In contrast, most of us rely on coffee to give a short-term boost to our performance. And it works – at least for a while. One or two cups of coffee contain enough caffeine to reduce drowsiness and fatigue, as well as improve mood, alertness and productivity. In one study (published in 2000 in *Ergonomics*) of 12 experienced navigators, caffeine enhanced some aspects of their performance – such as a visual search of a chart. However, it did not enhance their ability to solve problems.

But caffeine's effect declines, or at least plateaus, with increasing consumption, and overnight caffeine deprivation leads to fatigue. We also rapidly develop a tolerance to caffeine and need more and more to gain the benefits. Yet high consumption can also produce anxiety, tremor, stomach upsets and so on. Most people find that between 10 and 15 cups of brewed coffee, but in some as few as five, a day can produce symptoms that mimic anxiety. In one case, a patient complained of suffering from severe anxiety that did not respond to tranquillisers. Doctors were stumped until they discovered that he drank 50 cups of coffee a day. There is no need to stop drinking coffee. Just think about how much you are drinking. Moreover, remember that cola drinks, tea and many performance-enhancing drinks contain caffeine.

Eat to beat fatigue

We are, largely, what we eat. Therefore, if we live on junk food, we should not be surprised that our performance suffers – not to mention the health problems we store up for ourselves. A poor diet contributes to fatigue, for example. Therefore, it follows that you can boost your energy levels by changing your diet to make it more nutritious. Hence, you might ensure that you get most of your calories (the Government's independent advisory group suggests 65 per cent) from carbohydrate-rich foods, such as pasta, bread, potatoes and beans. Complex carbohydrates – in other words, not sugar – slowly release sugar into your bloodstream, supplying your muscles and brain with the energy needed to avoid fatigue and help you work at your full potential.

At the time of writing, the Government suggests that 35 per cent of our calories should come from fat – such as spreads low in saturated fat, olive oil and oily fish – and the rest from calories from protein-rich foods such as pulses, chicken and fish. (Some cardiologists and nutritionists suggest that fat should contribute less than this to our calorie intake, perhaps 25 per cent.) Also, ensure that you eat at least five portions of fruit and vegetables a day. This should help you maintain adequate levels of vitamins and other minerals. Some people who eat poor or unbalanced diets may need supplements. (Of course, it is more important to eat a balanced diet.)

There are several other things you can do to help beat fatigue:

- avoid sugar-loaded foods, such as chocolate bars or drinks. The rapid rise in blood sugar gives you an initial mental lift. However, as your body tries to compensate, sugar levels fall rapidly, leaving you feeling even more fatigued than before
- avoid large lunches, which can make you sluggish in the afternoon, especially if you drink alcohol as well
- do not be tempted to skip meals. Some people find that eating several small meals is better than a single large meal. Other people find they perform best after eating a single large meal. You should try to discover what works best for you
- in particular (yes, Mother was right), eat your breakfast. If you do not you may experience a rapid decline in blood sugar levels. This underlies the mid-morning crash and undermines your concentration and performance.

Find the time for exercise

Many people say that a lack of time is the main reason why they do not exercise. Yet, regular exercise can reduce the pressure on the rest of your schedule by helping you feel mentally alert and physically healthy. This means that you are better placed to make the most of your time and be at your most productive. Think of it as an investment: a few hours invested each week in exercise may increase your productivity during the rest of the time. The same principle applies to meditation and relaxation (see below). Activities such as t'ai chi and yoga (see Chapter 8) allow you to meditate while exercising.

The ultimate way to increase your time

Exercise may well be the ultimate way to increase your time over your lifetime. Estimates vary, but remaining physically fit may reduce the risk of premature death by around 40 per cent. You will also look and feel better. Scientific studies now show that, for example, jogging for two hours a week may reduce anger, alleviates depression and enhances feelings of calmness and vigour. On the other hand, the stress-beating benefits of exercise depend on your approach. For example, if you focus on your performance too much, you can actually feel more stressed when you leave the gym.

If possible, try getting up earlier, or make the most of lunchtime sessions that are offered at swimming pools and gyms. Alternatively, ask your partner to cook when you work out. Remember that three 20-minute sessions of moderate exercise a week keeps you fit. Even allowing for showering and changing, that is just 45 minutes each time you work out. There are 168 hours in a week; you need less than three to stay fit.

If even this seems too much, you may be able stay fit without regular trips to the gym. The US Centers for Disease Control and Prevention and the American College of Sports Medicine recommend accumulating at least 30 minutes of moderate-intensity physical exercise over the day. So you could add a 10-minute walk to the office, perhaps by getting off the bus a couple of stops early, and a 20-minute walk at lunchtime to meet the target. Alternatively, you could cycle to work instead of driving, for example.

There is really no reason why we should not all find the time to exercise. However, you need to find something you enjoy. Not everyone wants to go to an aerobics class or run a marathon, but there will almost certainly be some form of exercise you will enjoy – you may just need to experiment to find it. Ask your local library or sports centre for details of classes and clubs in your area.

Meditation and relaxation

Meditation and relaxation are undoubtedly very effective ways to bolster your defences against stress and increase your alertness, as well as improve concentration and mind-body co-ordination. And there are numerous ways to reach these goals, including classic meditation, relaxation, yoga and t'ai chi (see Chapter 8).

Meditation

People who meditate regularly often report that their academic performance, interpersonal relationships and marital satisfaction improve. Other studies find that meditation boosts IQ, improves creativity and relieves stress-related disease, including raised blood pressure, anxiety and insomnia (see *The Which? Guide to Managing Stress*). As such, meditation is a valuable part of time and life management.

Classically, meditation involves sitting serenely on a mat, legs crossed and focusing on your breathing or a saying (mantra) for 20 or 30 minutes two or three times a day. Transcendental meditation (TM)★ requires shorter sessions of between 15 and 20 minutes. This may seem a considerable time commitment in a busy life. However, meditators usually find that taking 40 or 60 minutes a day to meditate helps them to achieve more with less effort – which is the ultimate aim of time and life management. Moreover, meditation helps you cope with stress – a major time-waster.

To learn to meditate correctly, you really need to seek instruction from a teacher. However, you can try meditation for yourself before investing time and money on a course. Find somewhere quiet. Sit comfortably: this does not need to be the full, cross-legged lotus position – a chair is fine. You need to ensure that you are able to sit still for around 20 minutes without being distracted by cramps and other aches and pains.

Now breathe deeply. Meditation teachers emphasise that most people tend to breathe into their chests instead of their abdomen. The teachers argue that by concentrating on breathing into the abdomen, we can learn to breathe slowly and deeply in stressful situations. Imposing this internal control seems to help meditators master external stresses. (In other words, it helps develop an internal locus of control – see Chapter 1.) As a result, stress and difficult situations are less likely to be overwhelming and reduce productivity. This may be one reason why meditation makes people more efficient and effective.

Now focus your attention – which, as anyone who has tried meditation knows, is much easier said than done. TM practitioners use a mantra – a personal phrase or saying given to them by their teacher. However, for this experiment, choose your own mantra. It does not have to be an exotic phrase. Any simple, non-emotive word will do, even if it is nonsense. The aim is to focus your attention on a single point. Repeat the phrase over and over in your mind. If your mind starts to wander bring it back to focusing on the mantra. The aim is to focus your mind on the repeated word. This brings your attention down to a single point and it is this, meditators believe, that is the key to meditation's benefits.

Alternatively, you could also try focusing on the motion of your breath in and out of your nose and mouth. You could also focus on a candle flame or crystal. These all concentrate your mind and exclude distractions.

However, maintaining concentration for 20 minutes is far harder than it sounds. You will probably find that your mind wanders off. Just accept these ramblings and re-focus your attention on the subject. Do not become annoyed with yourself.

If you find that this works for you, it is best to find a teacher. Many adult education centres now run relaxation and meditation courses. TM is taught at 50 centres across the UK. However, while TM has the highest profile, it is not the only approach. The Buddhist Society★ can put you in touch with teachers of traditional Buddhist and Zen meditation.

Relaxation

If meditation does not appeal – and it does not suit everyone – you could try relaxation techniques. Find a quiet room where you can sit in a comfortable chair or lie down. Take the phone off the hook and turn the lights off. Make yourself comfortable and wear comfortable clothes. The room should not be too hot or cold.

Think about your breathing. Most of us breathe shallowly, using the upper parts of our lungs. However, to relax, you need to breathe deeply and slowly without gasping. Put one hand on your chest and the other on your abdomen. Breathe normally. You may find – especially if you are tense – that the hand on your chest moves, while the hand on the abdomen and remains almost still. The hand on your stomach should rise and fall, while the one on your chest hardly alters.

You can then use one of two approaches: *progressive muscular relaxation* or *tension-relaxation*. Whichever of the techniques you choose, try to relax every day. You might find that first thing in the morning is the best time. Try to avoid using these techniques last thing at night, as you will probably find yourself falling asleep. Equally, do not try them after a meal – when your stomach is full, blood diverts from your muscles to your stomach, and trying to relax tense muscles when blood is diverted from them can cause cramps. Furthermore, relaxation, like meditation, increases your awareness of your body's functions, and a full stomach can prove a distraction.

During *progressive muscular relaxation*, you aim to relax each part of your body in turn. After a few deep breaths, start at your toes. Say to yourself: 'My toes are tingling . . . They are becoming numb . . . they are getting heavier and heavier . . . the tension is draining away,' and so on. Then repeat this with your calves. Then move to your thighs and gradually work your way up your body. Once you reach your forehead, rest for a few minutes before standing up.

During *tension-relaxation*, you tense – slowly, gently and gradually – a muscle for around ten seconds before relaxing. You repeat this three times. The key is to tense your muscles slowly, gently and gradually. Inhale as you tense each muscle, breathe normally as you keep it tense, and then exhale as you relax. You are trying to relax, not build up your muscles. Then rest for a couple of minutes and then tense and relax the muscle another three times. After another rest, tense and relax the muscle a final three times. In other words, you need to tense and then relax the muscle nine times. Then move on to the next part of the body.

You can try tension-relaxation by putting your hands by your side. Inhale and clench your fist as hard as you can. Hold for ten seconds, while breathing normally. Now exhale and slowly relax. Alternatively, try the shoulder shrug – which is useful if you spend hours using a keyboard. Inhale and shrug your shoulder as high as you can. Hold for ten seconds while breathing normally. Now exhale and slowly let your shoulders drop. Another useful exercise to use at work is to drop your head forward until your chin touches your chest. Hold for ten seconds, and then slowly move the head to one side towards your shoulder. Hold for ten seconds, and then slowly move your head to the other side. However, do not roll your head or put your head right back. This can damage your spine.

Most people who teach tension-relaxation exercise believe that you should master each muscle before moving to the next. This means that you may take two or three months before you can work around your whole body. It is worth making the effort. After a while, you will come to recognise which muscles are tense. Most of us live for several years with considerable muscle tension, to which we have become used. However, once you know that a muscle is tense you can target it with an appropriate exercise.

Some days you will find it easier to relax than others – but do not give up. After a while, relaxation sessions will become part of your everyday life. You will feel less tired and less stressed. Your productivity will improve and you will be able to make the most of your time. However, you have to give relaxation a chance.

Simply put, maintaining a healthy body, through diet and exercise, avoiding fatigue and relaxing can improve your performance, which makes implementing time and life management much easier. Maintaining a healthy body and avoiding fatigue also directly increases the amount of time available to us. Counter fatigue and you may be able to get up earlier. Exercise and you will live longer. Staying healthy offers you the foundation that will allow you to use the time and life management strategies in this book to their full potential. Looking after yourself is, therefore, a central part of time and life management.

Chapter 7

Time and life management at work

Look at your desk. What does it tell you about the way you work? Is it covered in paper? Or do you just keep the essentials close to hand? Do piles of papers surround you at work? Is your in-tray always overflowing? Do you have a phone directory-worth of people to call back? Do you run around 'fire-fighting', continually facing deadlines? Do you take work home with you? Do you feel stressed? Do Post-It notes surround your computer screen?

If even a couple of these descriptions apply to you, you probably need radically to rethink the way you manage your time at work. You do not help anyone by losing control of time. If you do, your productivity – and, therefore, your company's – falls, your stress levels rise and your health suffers. And if you need to spend more time at work, you are likely to go home exhausted, and so your entire life is thrown out of balance. Most of us spend more time at work than with our families. So, if we get time management right at work, the rest follows more easily.

Productivity and stress

When most people think of time management, they usually think of ways to improve productivity at work. Certainly, employers increasingly expect their staff to produce more and more in less and less time. This is underlined in a survey conducted by the Institute of Management in 1999, which found that most of the 5,000 executives interviewed felt under time pressure. Eighty per cent cited tight deadlines as the main reason that they worked long hours. Indeed, more than half needed to work long hours to find the time to think strategically. However, it is interesting to note that during the three-day week during the 1970s, productivity dropped by only a few per cent rather than the 40 per cent you might have expected. Hours worked and productivity are not necessarily directly related.

However, as with everything, there is a price (opportunity cost – see Chapter 1) to pay for spending more time at work. The same survey suggested that almost three-quarters of executives said that working long hours undermined their health. Even more said that their family relationships, as well as their social and leisure time, suffered. Working long hours is not even good news for the company. Two-thirds felt that working long hours compromised morale and productivity. Many other studies confirm that time pressure is a leading cause of stress at work. All this means that stress is a pervasive problem in the modern workplace – as highlighted in *The Which? Guide to Managing Stress* (Which? Books).*

On the other hand, we need to keep problems posed by work in perspective. Most people are relatively satisfied with their jobs. A 1999 survey by the National Centre for Social Research found that around 80 per cent of workers are either very or fairly satisfied with their job and find their manager's performance either good or very good. Nevertheless, almost everyone can benefit from increasing their productivity by better management of their time at work. This means thinking about your efficiency and effectiveness.

Efficiency and effectiveness

Many people use the terms 'efficiency' and 'effectiveness' interchangeably. However, they differ subtly. You can be efficient without being effective and *vice versa*. If you are efficient, you perform the task in hand correctly. If you are effective, you perform the correct task. Therefore, you can do the right task (effectiveness) poorly (inefficiency). And you can do the wrong task (ineffectiveness) well (efficiently). Clearly, to maximise your productivity at work and to make the most of your time generally, you need to be both effective and efficient.

Improving your efficiency and effectiveness at work will reduce your stress levels as well as increasing the quality and quantity of your work. At the same time, you will find that you have more time for your friends and family. This chapter offers some practical ideas and resources from which you can choose the elements that work for you

– a time and life management tool kit that you can call on as and when you need it.

You may need to experiment to find which of these techniques suit you and your job. However, once you have built your time and life management tool kit and implemented the changes (see Chapter 3) you should work smarter rather than just harder. In other words, you will be more effective and more efficient.

Get organised

'One of these days, I'm going to get organised, just as soon as I have the time' is a common comment around the workplace. However, unless we make changes, we may never have the time to get organised. Even preparing to change takes time. So you need to organise yourself. This means, for example, introducing techniques to improve time and life management one step at a time – often changes at home and work fail because we try to do too much too soon.

In order to implement changes, you may have to work late or put in extra time over a weekend. This does not contradict all that has been said about keeping your life in balance. Rather, working a few hours over a weekend to develop a standard operating procedure for a task that you will then be able to delegate regularly may mean paying the opportunity cost of missing some time with your family. However, look on it as an investment. Freeing yourself from that task could allow you to spend more time with your family in the future. Indeed, preparation is the key to implementing many of the time and life management strategies, which should help enhance the productivity of you and your staff. (Such strategies are outlined in this chapter.)

Just what do you do?

Most of the tips below help you work efficiently. However, you need to begin by considering your effectiveness. In other words, you need to know that you are doing the right job. Think about your position in the organisation in which you work, perhaps by referring to your organisational chart or your job description. Think about who influences your day-to-day life – for example, your boss or clients; the people who work for you; and your peers. How do they interact to meet the company's and, more particularly, your department's aims? (It is also worth noting that your team members', colleagues' and bosses' bad habits can damage your effectiveness. You could try noting down the number of times that someone else's lack of planning undermines your plans. You can then try to do something to address these problems.)

Then consider your primary purposes at work – you should have no more than three. In other words, ask yourself: what is it that I do that moves my department and, therefore, company towards its organisational aims? And consider your areas of responsibility. What aspects do you control? Remember that you may have accumulated some of your responsibilities over the years, some of which are outside your job description. If there are a number of these, you might want to discuss reassigning them or redefining your job description. (This is another good reason to hone your negotiating skills – see page 106: you might be able to negotiate a salary increase.) Your responsibilities should really fit in with your primary purpose. Thinking about these issues should help clarify your effectiveness.

Tips on tackling paperwork

Despite the much-heralded paperless office, most of us are in danger of being smothered in piles of paper that cover our desks, cascade on to the floor and fill banks of filing cabinets until they burst at the seams. However, most of this is little more than clutter. A study by Stanford University found that almost 90 per cent of filed paper is never looked at again and, inevitably, many of us can never find those items we require when we need them in the remaining 10 per cent. So, what can you do to tackle paperwork?

Use your in-tray

Reserve your in-tray for other people to leave papers for your attention. It should not be a pending tray. Once you touch an item in your in-tray, it should never go back. In other words, do not use the in-tray as a surrogate filing cabinet and do not use it to remind you of your high-priority items.

If you reserve the in-tray for other people's use, you will see when there is something new that you have to deal with. So regularly, perhaps once, twice or even more times a day (obviously depending on how rapidly it fills up) sort through the in-tray and move each item into one of three other trays:

- **pending** This tray holds things you do not need to do now
- **urgent** These are things that you need to deal with quickly. (But remember to update your pending tray regularly and move items into the urgent tray)
- **out** Lets the post staff or your PA know that you have finished with a document. Make sure that your out-tray is emptied at least once, but ideally twice, a day.

Keep a reading file

Most of us now have to read vast numbers of journals, papers and reports in order to stay up-to-date with developments at work and in our profession. One approach to managing this is to skim a document and decide if it is something you need to read now. If not, and yet you think that the document is worth reading, either tear out the article, photocopy it or stick it into a reading file. If you receive PDF (portable document format) files and you are happy reading on screen, print out the first page as a reminder.

In general, put new documents at the bottom or back of your reading file so the oldest documents are at the top (unless, of course, you need to read others soon). You can then pull some papers out of your reading file to read at home, between appointments or on the train. If you find the reading file begins to budge at the seams, go through and weed out anything that appears peripheral. In extreme cases, you can simply bin everything before a certain date. Many time and life management gurus suggest that your PA or a colleague can read things for you and highlight appropriate sections. However, as mentioned in Chapter 5, you may want to keep this central task for yourself. Information is, increasingly, influence.

Throw out old report drafts

If you need to maintain a data or paper trail, keep previous versions of the report on disk rather than as hard copy. Indeed, you might be surprised how many drafts of old reports lurk in the depths of your filing cabinet. Consider how much of an information morgue you need. Is it necessary to keep reports dating back 18 months? Will three months suffice? That includes work you originated – keep copies on a floppy or zip disc rather than as hard copy.

Think before you file

Obviously, you need to archive items that you are legally obliged to keep, such as information for tax purposes, contracts, regulations and so on. However, does it really have to be stored in your office? Is there anywhere else on site that you can store this information? How about investing in some space at a commercial archive? Unless you need to access this information regularly, it might be worth seeing whether you can store it elsewhere.

You need to be critical with what is left. Look at every piece of paper or file and ask yourself whether you really *need* it. Only keep the paperwork if it helps you do your job and you cannot access it easily in some other way. Do you really need that newspaper clipping in the office, when the company or library has a copy? How many times will you refer to it? If it is important to you personally, consider keeping it at home.

Think how you file

You need to develop a flexible system that meets your needs. That may not be the traditional filing cabinet with hanging files. Some people prefer box files. Others use binders with dividers and, if needed, wallets. It really depends on you, your work and your style. The aim is to be able to access the information you need quickly using a system that is flexible enough to meet any changes in your work.

Think before you dictate

Formal letters have their place. However, do you really need to dictate a letter for everything? Would an email suffice? Writing an email is often quicker than dictating a letter. What about a phone call? What about a hand-written response? In some cases, a hand-written note is more effective – it seems more personal.

Learn effective writing

Writing a memo, report and letter in clear, unambiguous English is a great time-saver for the person who has to read it. It also saves you time: how often do you need to explain something because it is unclear in your report? Numerous books can help you write effective business English. In essence, the key is to avoid jargon and stick to simple sentences.

However, before you can write clearly, you need to have your idea clear in your mind. This means, once again, taking the time to prepare. Plan what you are going to say and how you are going to say it before your finger hits the key. You could ask a colleague or your boss to comment on the outline before you begin.

Have a clear desk policy

Some companies, perhaps for confidentiality reasons, operate a clear desk policy. Each desk has to be clear of paper at the end of each day; failure to achieve this may even be a disciplinary offence. Having a clear desk policy also helps you stay in control of your paperwork. It forces you to file effectively and efficiently.

Make sure you really need every report and memo

Make sure that every report you ask your staff to write is really needed. Sometimes people write reports through habit rather than necessity. Is a weekly sales report needed? Would a monthly summary offer a better overview? Is a memo needed? Would an email or phone call suffice? Does everyone in the company need to be cc'd on your emails? You need to think about every aspect of the hard copies and virtual documents that you and your team members generate. Moreover, you should regularly consider the distribution list for reports and journals. In some cases, the recipient may prefer to be sent an executive summary. He or she can always ask for a copy of the full report if necessary.

Include brief instructions on each form

Most companies require form-filling for expenses, time sheets, purchase recommendations and so on. After considering whether the form is really needed, consider including abbreviated instructions on each form. This will cut down the number of errors and the need to remind people how to use each form, especially if they do not complete them regularly.

Consider using a job bag

Many advertising, public relations and media companies use job bags. These are – sometimes literally – bags or folders that contain every email, letter, meeting report, work in progress costing and so on concerning the project. Everything goes into the job bag and, at the end of the project, the critical paperwork is sorted out and archived. You could use a similar approach.

Ask everyone who is working on a project to use the job file. On the front, clip a job sheet that summarises the tasks, people involved internally and externally (with contact numbers), completion dates for each stage and the final deadline as well as a space for notes. This keeps all the paperwork in one place, while allowing you to access all the documents if someone is absent.

Consider using follow-up files

Often you may need to follow up a lead, customer or creditor after a set time. Remembering to do this can be difficult. However, you can remind yourself in several ways:

- simply mark the date in your diary
- use a card index in date order
- use the alarm function on your computer.

Some self-employed people use a follow-up file for invoices. They put the invoice into one of 31 numbered files (one for each day of the month). They then know which invoices are due 14 days or a month later, according to their business terms. The same principle could apply to sales leads by keeping the contact report in the file.

Think about binning the Post-Its

Post-It notes are often indispensable. They allow you to annotate books and magazines without damaging them. They allow you to write notes to your assistant. But do you ever scribble a note on a Post-It and then forget to transfer it to your 'to do' list? Have you managed almost to paper your wall with Post-It notes? If so, you are probably a Post-It addict. The only answer is to do without Post-Its for a month or so until you get back in the habit of using your 'to do' list.

The art of delegation

Effective delegation is one of the cornerstones of effective time and life management at work. If you are a manager, you should remember that that is what you are employed to do. A manager achieves objectives *by co-ordinating the tasks of others*. This means that effective, efficient delegation is a core management skill. Indeed, effective, efficient delegation allows you to optimise your team, by allowing everyone to play to their strengths, while freeing the time for you to focus on your key priorities. Moreover, effective, efficient delegation develops your staff's skills and improves your team's motivation. In today's climate of flatter, thinner organisations people tend to delegate up and across as well as down, which encourages co-operative working relationships.

You can begin by looking through your 'to do' list. Are you sure that you need to do everything yourself? Do you need to make all those routine calls or write those memos? You can probably delegate many of these tasks. (But do not delegate only the jobs you hate.) However, keep hold of the tasks that have the greatest impact on your principal priorities.

Nevertheless, you need to manage, control and co-ordinate the delegation carefully. Compile a list of the tasks you have delegated, complete with the deadline and the name of the person to whom you have delegated responsibility. In some cases, especially if you have to do a number of rather dull jobs, it might be worth putting the chart up as a gentle reminder. (You will gain kudos among your colleagues by being seen to shoulder some of the dull tasks yourself.) This helps ensure that everyone understands what is expected of them. In other words, effective delegation means clearly establishing each delegated project's boundaries and each individual's responsibilities.

Moreover, when you delegate, it is important to consider the team's dynamics and technical competence. Some people may be better suited for certain tasks than others. On the other hand, you may deliberately decide to delegate tasks that stretch a member of your team. Although, if you do this, you should be prepared for mistakes, it is still a useful way to develop your team and free time for yourself in the future. The time and money you invest in training the person yourself or sending him or her on a course should pay off in increased productivity. In addition, your department's or section's increased productivity will reflect well on your management status.

Once you begin delegation, it can become part of your office culture. For example, all the reports that you are responsible for should include action points, a completion date and the name of the person working on the project. You could also consider formulating a standard operating procedure (SOP) for routine delegated tasks. SOP defines the process (usually step-by-step), reporting systems, outcome and quality assurance that you need to complete the task. The SOP should also include an action plan, stating what to do if things go wrong. By using an SOP, you should need to show someone how to perform the task only once. Moreover, writing an SOP forces you to dissect what you do, which often highlights ways in which you can improve efficiency. However, it is usually best to ask the person who routinely performs a task to write the SOP.

Of course, you need to trust your colleagues to get on with the job. Avoid the temptation to keep peering over their shoulders to see how things are going. On the other hand, you will need to provide feedback and review at the appropriate time. Moreover, link this increased responsibility with reward – financial or otherwise. Effective delegation is more of an art than a science. Nevertheless, the rewards in terms of more effective time and life management, a motivated staff and a more productive department can be marked.

Using the phone

Obviously we all know how to use the phone. It is indispensable and its importance is still growing. Twenty years ago, we spent an average of seven hours a year on the phone. Today, it is 120 hours. However, the fact that we use the phone several times a day does not necessarily mean that we use it to its greatest advantage.

Consider voicemail. Voicemail is a useful way to screen calls and to ensure that you do not miss an important call. To make the most of this valuable tool, you could try the following tips.

(1) Keep your voicemail message updated. If you are going to be out of the office for a couple of weeks, say so. However, be wary of doing this if you work from home, for security reasons. You could try using one of the commercial answering services during the time that you are away. You can access your messages while away and then call back.

(2) When recording or leaving a message, state clearly who you are and, if necessary, the name of your department. Fielding someone else's messages is a waste of time.

(3) When recording or leaving a message, keep it brief. You might want to repeat any numbers and leave any extraneous information to the conversation.

(4) If possible, leave an emergency number on your answerphone message, but ensure that someone will be able to take the call.

(5) Think hard before recording a humorous message. It is often hard for people to leave a serious message after a supposedly funny introduction.

It is worth making the effort to utilise this facility, although it is not universally popular. The answerphone is, according to one survey, the third most-hated aspect of business life. Only traffic wardens and junk mail are held in less regard. Perhaps the most telling statistics are that 70 per cent of callers hang up without leaving a message and that 45 per cent of voicemail systems are turned off within a year.

Using the phone more effectively

Voicemail shows that while we may be living through a telecommunications revolution, many of us do not make the most of it. Many people still fax or phone, when email would be quicker and cheaper. In addition, consider conference calls. These are easy to set up, save travel time and yet are often not used to their full potential. (If you use these services, remember to let people know who is speaking. Do not rely on them recognising an electronically distorted voice. Just saying, for example, 'Mark here' or even just 'Mark' before you talk will suffice.)

The growth in telecommunications also means that we often need to make several calls during the day. As a result, it is often worth performing similar tasks – a number of telephone calls and correspondence, for example – at one time. First thing in the morning is often a good time to make calls. People are more likely to be in their offices. And crossing off several items from your 'to do' list gives you a psychological boost.

Nevertheless, it is also easy to become caught up in the hype surrounding the telecommunications revolution. About 43 per cent of the population in the UK now owns a mobile phone. But how many of us really need a mobile phone? Do you need a mobile phone or a pager to keep in touch because someone is ill? Do you genuinely need it because you are on the road and need to stay in touch with the office? Alternatively, do you use it to call your partner when you leave the office at your usual time to tell them that you are on your way home? Do you use it to arrange to meet a friend?

Keep a note of how many times and for what reasons you use your mobile or pager over a couple of weeks. How many of those were essential calls that could not have waited? How many could you have made from a public telephone box? Now look at your mobile phone bill . . .

Moreover, remember that mobile phones have an off switch. Today mobile phones often impinge on time that our predecessors would have used to think. O.K., you could miss a call. But, based on your phone log, what is the chance of it being important? There is always the answer service. On the other hand, if you regain the time that you may once have used to think without interruption, it could lead to an innovative strategic idea. Trivial interruptions on your mobile phone are at least as intrusive as someone entering your office.

Ergonomics

You spend more time at your desk than in your home, but how much thought have you given to the design of your office compared to the time you spent planning your latest DIY project? Muscle tension is a common symptom of stress and poor posture while at work, especially in sedentary jobs in poorly designed offices, only makes matters worse. Too often, the only exercise we get during the day is the movement of our fingers and hands over the keyboard and mouse pad.

This combination of stress-related muscle tension and poorly designed offices compromises our health, limits productivity and makes us less time-efficient. It can also lead to musculo-skeletal problems, such as back pain and repetitive strain injury, which in the UK result in more than 11 million working days being lost each year and which cost industry over £5 billion. Clearly, thinking about ergonomics and office design is a valuable way to help you make the most efficient use of your time at work.

However, you do not necessarily need to hire an expensive ergonomic or *feng shui* consultant to redesign your office. There are some simple steps you can take to make your working environment less stressful and more time-efficient. For example:

(1) try to ensure that you have sufficient desk space. For example, if needed and if possible, have your computer on a separate desk

(2) when you are designing your office or workspace, keep frequently used books, CD-ROMS, materials and supplies (such as pens and staplers) nearby

(3) keep a filing system with regularly used information nearby. You can, if you have the space, have another filing system further away for less commonly used files

(4) maintain good posture. When you sit, try to keep your shoulders and head in a straight line and drop your shoulders. Sit upright at your desk with your feet on the floor. Placing a cushion at the base of your spine helps you maintain good posture. Poor posture may contribute to repetitive strain injury

(5) ensure that you have adequate lighting. This may mean experimenting with, for example, desk lighting

(6) adjust your computer screen so that you can see it when you look straight ahead. Position the screen so that you avoid glare from a window or light

(7) move your keyboard so that you are not hunching or lifting your arms. Your elbows should be at right angles and your feet on the floor. Think about buying a wrist support or, better still, one of the new ergonomic keyboards – once you get used to the new layout these are more comfortable to use. The ergonomic keyboards may also increase your typing speed

(8) get a comfortable, supportive desk chair

(9) if you use the phone a lot, use a headset instead of clamping the phone between your head and shoulder

(10) if you use a keyboard continually, take a five-minute break every 30 to 60 minutes: use tension-relaxation exercises (see page 128) to ease stiff shoulders and neck. Stand and walk around. Watch for signs of muscle tension. In addition, use tension-relaxation exercises at the first sign of tension.

Noise pollution

Noise pollution is increasingly recognised not only as a nuisance that makes it hard to think and undermines productivity, but also as an overt health hazard. It is hard enough to work effectively and make the best use of your time without the added pressure of heavy machinery running in the background, a jackhammer pounding away below your office window or the constant babble in a call centre. The Royal National Institute for Deaf People★ estimates that noise levels in around 88,000 workplaces are hazardous to hearing, which exposes 1.3 million employees to unacceptable risk. Essentially, if two people standing a couple of metres apart need to shout, then the workplace is dangerously noisy. The Association of Noise Consultants★ can help you assess noise levels and implement reduction strategies.

However, you should also be aware of the impact of lower-volume noise. While many noise specialists suggest that 85 decibels is the cut-off point for damage – someone shouting is roughly 80 decibels – people working long hours in an environment with noise levels lower than this may also suffer. So, use time and life management techniques to limit your exposure to these intrusive, stressful environments. You can also take this a step further. Many companies find that having a 'quiet' area helps improve productivity and encourages more effective use of their employees' time.

Stopping interruptions

Interruptions probably waste more time than almost anything else at work. Indeed, they present a particular problem because, by definition, you cannot plan for them. You could keep a record of how many times a day you are interrupted – and how many times you interrupt the people with whom you work. You can then categorise the interruptions and see if there is anything you can do to limit them. You could, for example, try the following:

- **expect the unexpected** Of course, you cannot really expect the unexpected. However, you can modify your time estimates to accommodate interruptions that you cannot avoid using some of the other tricks and techniques in this section. You may need to add anything from 10 to 50 per cent – so do your best to limit the interruptions. Keeping a time log (see Chapter 5) will help you estimate how much additional time you need

- **think about technology** If appropriate, use voicemail or an answer machine if you need some time uninterrupted by phone calls. Remember to turn your mobile phone off
- **get away from the office** Working at home, in another office, conference room or library – at least some of the time – minimises interruptions. However, ensure someone in the office knows where you are in case of an emergency. If you need to reflect or plan strategically, use your lunch hour to go to a local café, library or park where you cannot be interrupted. Again, turn the mobile phone or pager off. Finding time to reflect and plan is one of the key ways to enhance your creativity (see below)
- **keep people standing** Limiting the number of seats in your office discourages long visits
- **get in earlier or leave later than others** However, make sure that you leave earlier and arrive later to compensate
- **eliminate 'drop-in' visits** You can do this by using a visual barrier or shutting your door. In an open-plan office, you could pin a note up saying whether or not you want to be interrupted. At home, you may need to separate your workspace from family space and have a contract with your children that this is protected space. Some home workers rule that if the door is shut, they want privacy. On the other hand, one of the pleasures of working at home is seeing your kids grow up, so it is something you might not want to be too rigid about. You need to decide what is right for you
- **set ground rules** When a colleague interrupts, ask whether it is *essential* to deal with the problem immediately. If not, ask him or her to wait until the time is convenient for you (and remember to go back to that colleague). Do this a few times and interrupters will get the message. You can also set a time limit for each interruption
- **avoid small talk** Keep small talk until lunchtime
- **keep a clock visible and glance at it a number of times** Another approach is to set a timer on your watch or computer for five minutes. Push it when someone enters. When it goes off you have an excuse to end the meeting – just mention there is an

important call you have to make. If the interruption really is important, you can always ignore the alarm. And, of course, if the interruption is really warranted, give the person your undivided attention

- **do unto others as you would have them do to you** Try to interrupt other people less frequently. Ask yourself whether it can wait. Can you use email or a note instead – especially if there are several things to discuss? Often you will be engaged in a discussion that wastes both your time.

Despite implementing all these techniques, you will still be interrupted. Interruptions are a fact of life. So, change your attitude towards them. Add time to your estimate to compensate and try not to become annoyed.

Tips for taming modern technology

There is no doubt that modern technology has transformed business life. Whether this is for better or worse in terms of our life management more generally is less clear. In a 1998 survey of more than 400 managers, by BT and *Management Today* magazine, 36 per cent said that technology helped them integrate their lives better, although 35 per cent felt that technology made the imbalance worse.

Indeed, many people find that modern technology just means that you have more things making demands on your time. We do not just have an in-tray to contend with any more, we also have an incoming mail file – and it is bulging. Analysts expect the number of worldwide daily email messages to increase to an average of 18 billion in 2003, from five billion in 1999. (And sometimes it feels as if they are all for you.) Indeed, they expect that a quarter of all customer contact will occur online.

So, while you will need to face the IT revolution eventually, a few simple techniques can help you tame modern technology.

(1) Do not have a 'you have mail' dialogue box that pops up on to your screen each time an email arrives – it can be extremely distracting. Look through your inbox or run a 'flash session' to download your emails two or three times a day

(2) Send batches of email at a time rather than going online several times a day

(3) Many people now receive 50, 100 or even more emails a day. So remember, keep them brief. And do not expect an instant answer – neither should you send a response without due consideration. Prioritise your email in the same way as any other document. You can even use folders for the A-E priorities (see page 93). And you could suggest setting a benchmark – responding by noon the next day, for example. If you are dealing with clients, you could consider setting up an automatic response suggesting that you will deal with the problem within the deadline

(4) Use folders. Keep emails on different topics separate. For example, you may want to keep separate folders for all emails on a project, those for reading later and personal notes

(5) Do you really need to 'cc' this email? Do not copy people because you can. Do it because they *need* to see it

(6) Think about your membership of mailing lists, electronic tables of contents for magazines (e-TOCS) and e-zines. Do you really benefit? Unsubscribe from those that you no longer read

(7) Re-read your email before sending it. You may save time later by preventing mistakes. While email is relatively informal, accurate spelling makes the email look more professional. Despite its informality, email is a permanent record and it reflects on your professionalism just as much as a letter or phone call

(8) Use a filter to prevent spam (junk email). Other filtering software can scan emails for key words and then categorise according to priority or subject matter

(9) Ensure you write descriptive subject headings. These help you track your emails and encourage recipients to open messages

(10) Keep an address book. The program will insert the address and help you track your contacts

(11) Consider autoresponders for frequently requested information, such as price lists and directions, and when you are away on holiday. However, remember the warning over the voicemail messages if you work from home (see page 139)

(12) Do not bookmark every site you visit, just in case you need to find it some time. Create a holding folder. If you do not visit that site again in a reasonable time, bin it.

Managing meetings

Meetings are probably the biggest time-waster in any company. How many pointless, dull meetings have you been to that achieved absolutely nothing? How many times could an email or telephone call have succeeded just as well? How many times have you had to work late because a meeting overran? And how often have you experienced managers failing to manage meetings effectively? In a recent survey, some three-quarters of directors believed that the quality of board meetings could improve.

There are three cornerstones to managing meetings effectively. Firstly, ensure that the meeting is really needed. Secondly, if it is needed, ensure everyone is adequately prepared. Thirdly, during the meeting ensure that everyone invited has the opportunity to speak. (What is the point of inviting managerial wallflowers?) The techniques of transactional analysis (see Chapter 5) are especially useful for chairing and participating in meetings – especially if conflicts arise or if someone is not making the contribution that they should.

Here are a number of other, more specific, things you can do to manage meetings more effectively.

(1) Ideally, meetings are held to discuss and solve a defined problem. For example, a meeting may be appropriate to discuss strategies to improve sales or discuss more effective ways of communicating key messages. An overview or update about the latest sales figures may be more effective on paper – unless the meeting gives the opportunity to discuss and challenge, with the aim of improving efficacy and effectiveness. (That is one reason why many managers find the most useful part of a conference is in the bar or coffee room rather than in the didactic sessions. These informal sessions allow people to discuss and review as well as network.) Listening to a series of monologues is worse than just boring – it also wastes everyone's time. You could communicate the information at least as effectively on paper

(2) Ask yourself whether the meeting is really necessary – or ask your boss this, if he or she convened it. You could, for example, list each month's regular meetings. Now place them in order of importance in terms of meeting the objectives of your company and its departments. Could you do without the least important

25 per cent of these meetings? One of the most persuasive arguments against meetings is the cost. Point out that the two-hour meeting just requested involves ten people. Based on salaries of £40,000, the meeting will cost £48 for each person (assuming a working year of 235 seven-hour days) – a total of £480. Then there are overheads to consider. Question whether a meeting is really worth the expense. Bear in mind Benjamin Franklin's maxim, 'time is money'

(3) Circulate any critical documents well in advance. Reviewing and presenting information that people could have read in advance simply wastes everyone's time. However, ensure that people have the opportunity to raise issues that they did not understand or agree with

(4) Think about holding the meeting away from the office. Using a hotel meeting room might be more cost-effective if, for example, many of the team members are on the road and need to travel long distance to head office. It helps minimise interruptions and keeps people focused on the topic

(5) Think about using modern technology. Could you hold a virtual, rather than face-to-face, meeting? Meeting to discuss issues in person is now less necessary than it used to be. Most of us know about conference calls, video links and limited-access Internet or intranet (a local internet) chat rooms. But how many of us use them? While there are times when a personal approach is essential, in many cases a conference call will suffice

(6) Invite people on the grounds of 'need to know'. Limit invitations to the meeting to those people who really *need* to be involved and who can make an informed contribution. Do not feel you need to invite someone for the sake of politeness. This ensures that the people you have invited have something to contribute. Therefore, make sure they have the opportunity to speak, especially if you know that they are shy or are new to the group. If other people will be interested in or affected by the outcome, consider circulating detailed minutes and a summary of action points with deadlines

(7) Ensure every meeting you go to or chair has an agenda. You could keep a list on your computer of topics that you need to tackle. Hold a meeting only when you have enough on the list to form an agenda. Circulate an agenda before the meeting.

And during the meeting use your agenda to help keep things on track. To do this, set and share the time you have allocated to each topic. If you feel that this may be politically insensitive, write a rough timing by the side of each topic on your copy of the agenda

(8) Hone your skills as the chair. Managing meetings effectively relies on having a firm chair who can keep the meeting on track, without stifling discussion and debate. The key is to ensure that the topics discussed are relevant – and stop the discussion becoming too technical. Ask the speaker to define any terms with which the rest of the group may be unfamiliar. (You could also write these on a flip chart ahead of the meeting to save any blushes.) Chairing a meeting is not easy. It is often difficult, for example, to strike the balance between keeping the meeting on track and not stifling debate. However, it is a skill that comes with practice. Again, transactional analysis can help

(9) If you can, delegate the logistics. Ensuring that the meeting room is well stocked with audiovisual aids, pens, coffee and so on may be a waste of your time. However, it is your responsibility to use the audiovisual aids. If you are the chair, these are invaluable for summing up the main points. They will also help you or your secretary draw up the minutes

(10) Note the start and end time on the agenda that you circulate before the meeting. Schedule meetings that you want to keep brief towards the end of the day or just before lunch. If you want to keep the meeting on time, schedule it for Friday afternoon. Allow no more than five minutes for any latecomers, then start the meeting. Being late for meetings can become almost routine for some people

(11) Review the meeting's effectiveness. Did it achieve what it set out to? Is there an identifiable output? Do the minutes state who is required to do what by when? You can also use any coffee and lunch breaks to review the meeting's progress and bring it back on track.

Manage your boss

As every manager knows, you have to manage your boss as well as, if not better than, your staff. However, the right attitude and approach are essential to manage your manager effectively. This means understanding what your boss wants. So, try to discover his or her agenda and then tailor your ideas to fit – although you can push at the boundaries without breaking them. In time, you will bring your boss round to your way of thinking. Once you have established a comfortable relationship, you can become more controversial.

You should also make yourself, as far as possible, indispensable to your manager through your deeds rather than by just saying yes. So when you close a deal ensure that your boss knows that you are responsible – and drop some hints about how tough it was, backed up by a paper trail so that no one else can take credit. However, allow your boss to bask in some – and the key word is 'some' – of the reflected glory. This will make him or her more willing to listen to you and help you in the future.

You could also put yourself in your boss's place and try to see things from his or her perspective. This means trying to understand what motivates your boss. See whether any of the models outlined in Chapter 4 fit your boss. Is he or she a climber or an expert? Presenting your ideas in a way that fits into the boss's characteristics increases your chance of success.

You can also ask yourself what you would want from your staff if you were in your boss's position. Think about the reasons why your boss should welcome your idea. If you cannot come up with several good reasons, chances are that it will flop. You should also think about some possible criticisms and address these in advance. (Performing a SWOT analysis – see below – can help clarify these.) If possible, test the water before plunging in and choose your time carefully. However, there is one rule above all others when you manage your manager: only fight battles you think you can win.

An adult-to-adult relationship

Think back to the ideas discussed under transactional analysis. The idea is to have an adult-to-adult relationship with your boss, whatever your relative positions in the organisational hierarchy. This means that you need to know your motivational style (see Chapter 4) as well as your goals and ambitions (see Chapters 3 and 4). You also need to know about your boss as well as his or her style and goals. You then need to develop an adult-to-adult relationship that meets, as far as possible, your aims and agenda as well as those of your boss.

Thinking about your boss in this way will also highlight some issues causing conflict between you. You can then decide how to tackle these issues. Over time, you will build trust between yourself and your boss and have good lines of communication that allow you to maximise your productivity, move closer to your goals and minimise the impact of problems.

Finally, if you want something specific – training, for example – sell it to your boss as a business proposition, ideally with costs and timings. Make a strong case, showing him or her why it matters to the department's productivity and, therefore, how it benefits the company. Point out how new training will improve productivity, which should be simple if, for example, you want training in IT skills. Explain how you will soon catch up with any work you miss due to this improved productivity. Then make sure, once you get back, that your boss knows how it has made a difference. If you can prove – perhaps by keeping a log before and after – that the training has made a difference, he or she may well be more likely to consider any future requests.

Think 'outside the box'

The key to dealing with today's rapid pace of change – as well as minor challenges, such as the best way to implement time and life management – is to be creative. Management consultants call this 'thinking outside the box'. In other words, you may need to challenge established wisdom in order to implement ways to work and live more effectively.

Thinking outside the box means becoming a creative learner. According to Trix Webber, writing in *Career Development International*, this means questioning and possibly changing the way you look at a problem. She cites the example of a company with falling sales. Conventional (so-called 'single-loop' learning) would try to find more effective ways to market existing products. The 'double-loop' approach – thinking outside the box – would fundamentally rethink products and markets. Obviously, both are appropriate responses, depending on the particular circumstances and the problem you are trying to solve.

151

Nevertheless, the double-loop approach relies on being creative. In today's business world – and it does not matter what product or service you sell – creativity is the key to honing your competitive edge. Moreover, using your time creatively improves productivity by enabling you to get more done in less time. Managing your staff and your boss creatively reduces office politics – one of the greatest corporate time-wasters (and causes of stress). And examining your sales profile, your products and markets creatively enhances your bottom line.

At its simplest, creativity means bringing something new into existence. In many cases, this may be joining together two previously unconnected ideas. However, you may need to overturn what went before, rebel against your teaching and re-examine established ways of doing things.

For example, in 1663, Isaac Newton, then a student in Cambridge, stopped taking notes in the middle of a lecture. He left dozens of pages blank before beginning a new page *Quaestiones Quaedam Philosophicae* – Some Philosophical Problems. Michael White, author of a biography of the scientist, remarks that this 'marks the point at which Newton stepped away from tradition and began to question what he was taught'. That quest was to end with Newton changing our view of the material universe. Few of us get even close to having such a profound insight. But the idea of questioning established ideas applies at home, in the office and in life generally.

In other words, naturally creative people are, intellectually at least, independent. They are influenced more by their inner standards than those of the society or profession to which they belong. This means that working towards, and in line with, *your* values and principles could unleash your creativity.

Beyond brainstorming

A brainstorming meeting is the conventional approach to developing creativity at work. However, how many brainstorming meetings have you been to that failed to come up with anything of value? So how do you spark new ideas? There is no easy answer. However, a number of tricks can help you look at a problem from a different viewpoint, which is really the key to creativity.

- Carry a notebook with you. Often the best ideas come at the most unexpected times. The graph overleaf shows the results of a BT and *Management Today* survey that asked managers and directors where they have their best ideas. Just over a fifth had their best ideas either at the office or in a brainstorming session. The other 80 per cent or so had their best ideas away from the office. However, the best idea in the world is useless unless you can remember what it was. Carrying a notebook allows you to note these insights down. It is also a useful way to remember something or to make a note when you are reading a book or journal.

- Play – let your hair down. A child at play builds castles in the air, worlds of fantasy and daydreams – all are creative acts. However, many adults lose the ability to daydream. They feel embarrassed about the time they 'waste' on idle speculation. Certainly, for every idea that you manage to bring to fruition, you may waste 100 daydreams. But that one idea could change the world – or at least your life. However, expect to make a few false starts. And if you do not like calling them daydreams, consider them thought experiments – Einstein did.

- Laughter may also boost creativity, probably because it is often subversive. However, while humour can aid creativity, you will need to become serious as you try to decide if the idea is valid and the best means of implementation.

- Many artists find visiting a gallery stimulates ideas that they can use in their work. This is not plagiarism. Rather, looking at another artist's view helps them look at their current work with a new eye. And there is no reason why you cannot unleash your creativity in a similar way. Try visiting an exhibition by an artist you do not know. Or borrow a CD from a library by an artist you do not normally listen to. Again, this can help unleash your creativity.

- You can also try deconstructing a current problem. What is wrong with the current situation? From this, you can reverse-engineer. In other words, you begin at the problem and work backwards, examining each stage in the process that produced the current situation to discover what is going on. This approach is especially useful when you are looking at systems or business practices that have built up over time.

- If you cannot find an answer, try sleeping on it. Leonardo da Vinci, probably one of the most creative people of all time, often read his notes before going to sleep. Sometimes you may need a longer incubation period. Twenty years was the incubation period for both Darwin's *The Origin of Species* and Brahms' first symphony. During this 'incubation period', the subconscious works on the problem. So, if you cannot immediately find a solution, look again at the problem after a couple of days.

- Some companies find that changing the office layout also helps. It might seem a daft idea, but many companies find that changing the environment has a psychological effect, often bringing new insights into staid practices.
- Try mind mapping. This powerful technique is similar to focused

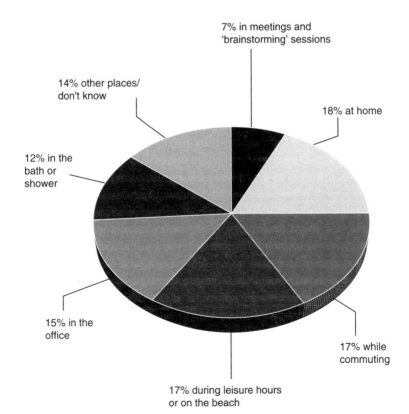

Where managers get their ideas

7% in meetings and 'brainstorming' sessions

14% other places/don't know

18% at home

12% in the bath or shower

15% in the office

17% while commuting

17% during leisure hours or on the beach

doodling and reflects the fact that the brain is not a computer that thinks linearly. You summarise the core concept – for example, a presentation's topic or the title of a report – at the centre of a page. Then decide the various topics or chapters that contribute to the idea. You then come up with key words and summary points linked to each of these topics. However, you can also doodle, use connecting arrows, symbols, coloured pens, drawings – whatever you want to feel your way around a theme. Several books, especially those by Tony Buzan, who invented the system, describe mind mapping in more detail. There are even computer programs that help you mind-map.

- Think laterally. In more than 60 books, Edward de Bono aims to enhance creativity by considering information in self-organising systems. From this, he developed a range of techniques – such as lateral and parallel thinking – that should help you unleash your creativity. His popularity shows just how effective many people find de Bono's approaches.

- Schedule time to think on your own without interruption. If you cannot find the time at work, try getting in early one day a week or rising an hour earlier on a Sunday morning.

- Perform a SWOT analysis. On a piece of paper, write down the Strengths, Weaknesses, Opportunities and Threats facing you. So, if you are thinking of ways to increase sales, look at your product's strengths and weaknesses (this means being honest about your product). Based on this, you need to look at the opportunities that strengths offer, both in your current and any possible market. You then consider the threats to the product from any rivals, changes in the marketplace and so on.

The key to creativity with a SWOT analysis, mind mapping, brainstorming and so on is to be non-judgemental. Do not offer opinions or judgements at first. Once you have exhausted your creativity, you can then decide which of the various ideas are practical – perhaps after leaving the matter for a couple of days. You can then develop a plan to maximise your opportunities in line with your strengths and minimise the threats arising from your weaknesses.

Leave your job at work – even if you work at home

These tools and techniques should help you perform more effectively at work. As such, they should reduce work-related stress and illnesses, and the time you need to move towards your personal goals and ambitions, as well as help you balance work, personal and financial commitments, and so on.

On the other hand, the march of modern technology makes it increasingly difficult to leave work behind us at the office. In a survey commissioned by BT and *Management Today*, 77 per cent of managers and directors said they now had the facility to email their office from home. Furthermore, 71 per cent were also equipped with PCs and modems, 58 per cent had laptop computers and 57 per cent fax machines at home. The problem with this technology is that few people make up the time they spend working at home. The gradual encouragement of the office at home makes it all too easy for your life to slip out of balance.

Nevertheless, as far as possible, leave your job at work – even if you work at home. Remember the fundamental rule of time and life management: as far as possible, ensure your life is in balance. We all need to work; we do not all need to become workaholics. So work smarter, not harder.

Chapter 8

Time and life management and your family

Most of us want to spend more time with our families and friends – it is one of the main reasons for wanting to learn time and life management techniques. However, these techniques are not just aimed at enabling you to spend more time at home; they also apply to your family life. Thinking about how you manage the time you spend with your family and how you plan your life together should increase the amount of quality time you spend with your family and friends.

════════════════

Sarah

Sarah Kennington is living proof that re-evaluating what matters to you can dramatically change your life. Sarah now hosts and edits *The Frugal Life,** a US-based e-zine and Internet site that aims to help people live within their means – a central theme of time and life management.

Once Sarah led a more conventional, career-focused life. In 1989, she was a single mother running a court-reporting firm. In 1990, she married and, after a year, she ran the company together with her new husband. However, by 1997, Sarah was, with her husband's sons, a mother of six.

'I realised how much of my boys' lives I had missed by working and made the commitment to stop working and come home,' she says. 'In order to do that I had to hire someone to fill my [role] and in doing so I gave up 80 per cent of my income.

'I knew things had to change in my household but wasn't quite sure how. We live on an acre of land in a 3,500-square-foot home. I was determined not to let that change,' Sarah recalls. 'I started going literally room to room and looking at the way I ran this home. I decided I could do it differently and my family would not suffer because of lack of income. We just needed to change the way we did things.'

Sarah began in the kitchen and re-thought everything from cooking to cleaning. 'Our grocery bill has been cut by two-thirds. I learned how to grow my own vegetables, how to can food, how to use all leftovers,' she says. 'Nothing goes to waste, not even the garbage which is now used for compost for the garden.' Sarah began buying almost all her clothes second-hand and traded work with other people. However, and critically, she has 'also learned how to wait for things'.

Sarah managed to take her family with her, by changing their expectations. 'My husband and older boys were willing to make the change because there is such a tremendous change in our lives by my being at home,' she says. 'My children would rather have me here than have the benefits that an extra income can bring. Now my husband will not only wear an Armani tie I buy at a garage sale, he brags about the fact that I bought it for $1.

'This change has not been easy,' Sarah admits. 'But like everything else in this life, with dedication and consistency anything can be achieved.' For example, she found going from being 'the boss and very busy and in adult conversation all day to being at home, not feeling "important" and losing the adult contact' difficult. 'It was a lifestyle change that I wanted to make but was difficult,' she says. 'Now, however, there isn't a sum large enough that would entice me to return to [my job]. What other people think no longer matters to me. I know what works best in my life and I know that my family is better.'

Radically changing her life brought Sarah true happiness – not a bad ambition to aim for, for any of us. 'I think the biggest surprise has been the feeling of content, true happiness. I thought I was happy before but the true feeling of having a life fulfilled was lacking,' she says. Sarah writes *The Frugal Life* to share her experiences with other people drowning in debt and with parents who are concerned about being at home to raise their children. She regards this as 'a God-given ministry' and donates the profits to charity.

'I no longer live to work,' Sarah says. 'When I wake in the morning I don't run to get dressed and worry that I'm not in the right fashion. When the phone rings and my child has forgotten his lunch, my first thought isn't "Oh, I've got a meeting today, let me see who can take care of him for me." My priorities are contained to the wellbeing of my family, my faith in God, love for my husband and betterment of myself.

'On the day that I take my last breath I know that I won't think, "Gosh, I should have spent more time in an office,"' Sarah concludes. 'I also know that there is no material thing that will go with me, nor will it matter. What will matter is how my children's lives have been moulded, that I have lived in a true state of happiness, that my husband has been truly loved and that God himself will pat me on the back and say, "Good job, my child."'

Keep a family planner

Sarah's story shows how you can step off the fast track and free up time for your family. But you will have to make sacrifices. Taking things as far as Sarah has, however, is a large step. In a less dramatic way, there are a number of things you can do to increase the quantity of quality time that you spend with your family.

One of the simplest is to keep a family planner. Nowadays, children take part in numerous extra-curricular activities and hobbies that occupy specific time slots. These may become part of your day-to-day habits. However, it is worth noting them down in a planner. It helps you know who does what when – and if there are any clashes with your commitments or those of your other children. You can also use the planner to see how you could free more time to spend together. You need to ask yourself and your children honestly whether the extra-curricular activity is really something that they want to do – or is it just a way to appease your conscience because you do not spend enough time with them?

Remember the idea of opportunity costs (see Chapter 1)? If you and your family want to spend more time together, the opportunity cost may be cutting down on some of these extra-curricular activities. (That includes your activities as well. Is the golf club more important than your children's sports and hobbies?) In this way, children begin to understand the opportunity costs associated with time – which should help them manage their time and their lives better as they mature.

In other words, you need to plan your time with your family in the same way that you plan your time at work. This will not necessarily compromise spontaneity. Just block the time off and, if you want to be spontaneous, decide what you are going to do at the last minute. Moreover, noting the time that you spend with your family is an excellent way to review whether your life is in balance and in tune with your personal values and philosophy. Taking this a step further and noting the activities that you and your family take part in over a couple of weeks can help you decide whether these activities reflect what matters to you. So, against each activity, ask yourself how satisfying and useful it was on a scale of one to ten. Of course, something may be useful and not especially satisfying – and *vice versa*. The aim for you and your family is to cut out those activities that are neither satisfying nor useful.

Create rituals to make the most of time

Spending more time with your family helps you rediscover the rituals that used to be part of the fabric of life – the same fabric that our hectic pace of life is slowly unravelling. Even religious festivals, such as Christmas and Easter (marked by public holidays, and a time to spend relaxing with family), have lost something through commercialisation. Every year people complain about how commercial Christmas has become, but how many of us do anything about it?

Even everyday rituals – going to a place of worship, eating together, playing games, reading, performing music, visiting friends or relatives – are dying out. These rituals allowed us to slow down in a hectic world. For example, they would have allowed you to spend time with your family, as well as develop and deepen your relationship with your partner. And consider the family meal. Twenty years ago, we spent an hour a day cooking and half-an-hour eating the family dinner. Now that is down to 20 minutes cooking and 10 minutes eating. Ten minutes affords little time to even enjoy your food, let alone develop any kind of relationship.

Perhaps inevitably, there has been a reaction against fast food at home. The Slow Food movement,* founded in Italy in 1986, now has some 60,000 members across 35 countries. The movement also has wider aims, such as to countering 'the "global taste village", which is standardising flavours and manipulating consumers'. The movement also aims to preserve our 'agro-industrial heritage'. That means defending biodiversity as well as the crafts and traditions surrounding food production.

Therefore, you could try bringing some of the rituals back into your daily life – as well as at Christmas, Easter, Chanukah, Diwali or whatever – in order to enjoy less frantic mealtimes. This does not need to be costly or complicated. Rather it means thinking about how you can make the time special – which, more often than not, just means spending time with your children. You could have a games evening, for example. Prepare some pizzas, perhaps, and play board games, charades and so on.

Similarly, instead of buying Christmas or Diwali decorations, you could make them with your children. You could also make more of a ritual of decorating the tree by creating some of the ornaments or by spray-painting pine cones. And at Easter, your children could make chocolate eggs (or paint real ones). Think back to your childhood. Was there anything that your parents or grandparents did that you enjoyed and that you could resurrect for your children? You may just breathe life into an old family tradition that can be handed down to the next generation and beyond.

You can also create rituals with your partner. For instance, try, if you can, to get out on a regular date. You could also consider taking up a hobby that you can share – this could be anything from learning French to learning to cook. If you share an ultimate ambition – such as owning a business – you could also share some of the learning tasks you identified during the skills audit.

Think about your children's expectations

Children's expectations are often a major source of anxiety for parents. Most parents feel guilty if they are unable to buy the toys their children want or cannot afford lavish birthday parties. However, it is worth remembering that advertising drives many of these expectations, directing children towards things they neither need nor really benefit from.

Companies see children, to an ever greater degree, as a soft touch. Indeed, between 1998 and 1999, companies launched 179 'innovative' new products for children – compared to 92 for adults. They would not make this investment unless they were sure that there was a market for the product. Yet how many crazes has marketing created

– from the hula-hoop to Pokémon – and how often have you spent a small fortune only to see a toy forgotten as the next product breaks on to the market? How many of the 'must-have' toys are gathering dust in the back of the wardrobe?

You cannot even escape at school. There is growing concern about the amount of 'sponsored' educational material that barely disguises its advertising agenda (for more detail about the involvement of businesses in education, see *The Which? Guide to Choosing a School*, from Which? Books).* Moreover, initiatives that allow schools to buy sports equipment if they consume vast amounts of snacks or buy computers if enough parents shop in a certain supermarket are none-too-subtle marketing tricks to reach your wallet through your children.

In a VSO survey (see Chapter 1), 84 per cent of respondents thought that the 'have it all' attitude is ruining our children's lives. Nevertheless, overcoming this indoctrination is difficult. You can try simply to explain why you cannot afford something. Try using the idea of opportunity costs outlined in Chapter 1. Even relatively young children often grasp that to buy one thing they may have to go without something else. In addition, it is important to stress that the fact you are not buying a particular product is not a reflection on the child. Rather, show your children that you value them above all else by spending time with them. You could even, somewhat brutally, explain that if they want the latest toy, you will have to spend more time at work.

You can also try cutting down on the amount of TV they watch. Many TV programmes now seem to be little more than extended advertisements for toys and computer games. Moreover, apart from driving expectations, watching excessive amounts of television is bad for children's health. For example, more children than ever before are now obese. Between 1972 and 1990 English and Scottish children showed a roughly twofold increase in weight for height in all age groups and both sexes. Research shows that an unhealthy childhood increases the risk of disease in later life (this tendency is called 'childhood programming'). Instead of letting them watch TV at every opportunity, encourage your children to swim, dance and play sports. As well as reducing their expectations with regard to whatever the latest craze happens to be, they will also become healthier.

Here are some other strategies that you can try to keep your children's expectations in check in an ever more materialistic world.

- Ask your children to make your cards and presents for birthdays, Mother's Day, Father's Day, Easter Diwali, Chanukah, Christmas or whatever. They will mean more to you – and help your child understand that you do not have to spend money to keep people happy. It will also help unleash their creativity.
- Try not to make promises that you cannot keep – even if that is the easy way out. It is all too easy, when your children hassle you for a new toy, to say yes. Of course, buy them a surprise every once in a while (and if you reduce the expense of regular, smaller items they nagged you for, it can be something special). However, do not promise them a visit to the toyshop or a holiday at a theme park to keep them quiet.
- Set your children financial limits. Encourage them to save some of their pocket money. They will then begin to understand that they cannot just have everything they want when they want it. It will also teach them the value of saving and the need to wait sometimes for something we want. At first, you might have to put up with a few sulks, especially if your children are used to you buying on demand, but they will soon adapt.
- Make your children buy the latest craze themselves. This will help them understand the idea of opportunity costs. (They have to forgo the opportunity to spend the money on something else.)
- Help them understand the difference between wants, needs and luxuries (see point 21 in Chapter 9).
- Pay them for extra chores. Apart from freeing up your time, this allows them to gain some extra money for something they want. It also helps to teach them the concept of opportunity costs.
- Think about a simple party with the old-fashioned games. Spending time with your children planning and preparing for a party is just as important as having a lavish party. Indeed, some parties seem to aim to impress the other parents rather than let the children have a good time. Block time out in the family planner to discuss and prepare for the party.

There is nothing wrong with buying children toys, games and comics. And we all want the best for our children. However, sometimes the best does not come in boxes, batteries not included. Time and life management aims to help you restore a sense of balance in your life, to liberate you from the need to work long hours to buy things that you and your children do not really want. So give your children the best – time with you.

Cut the clutter

Clutter makes life difficult and wastes time. However, many of us are surrounded by clutter that, to paraphrase William Morris, we do not know to be useful or believe to be beautiful. Certain clues may indicate that you are a clutter junkie.

- Do you store papers, bills and so on in stacks or stuffed into envelopes?
- Do friends admire your 'interesting' house?
- Do they ask: 'Where on earth did you get that?'
- Do you keep old magazines and papers that you never look at?
- Does your garage look like a waste tip?
- Do you hoard junk mail?
- Do you keep clothes your children have grown out of?
- Do you have a wardrobe full of clothes that were fashionable several years ago?
- Are your kitchen cupboards full of out-of-date foods?
- Are your kitchen cupboards full of paraphernalia you never use? For example, many people have juicers and fondue sets gathering dust in the depths of their kitchen cupboards.
- Is your bathroom cupboard full of cosmetics and skin care products that you never use?
- Look around you and in your cupboards and drawers. Are they full of things that you have not used for more than a year?
- Do you have a junk drawer full of old keys, vouchers, take-away menus and strange-looking pieces of metal that seem to have appeared from nowhere?

The more this sounds like you, the closer you are to being a clutter junkie. Decluttering can be difficult. However, over time, you realise that you did not really need all that stuff. (It also helps you focus your purchasing on what really matters.) Clutter really adds little to your life, hides the things that do matter and takes time to look after. Thoreau noted 200 years ago: 'I had three pieces of limestone on my desk, but I was terrified to find that they required to be dusted daily . . . and I threw them out of the window in disgust.'

Decluttering means that you can find the things that you really need more rapidly – which further frees your time for the things you really want to do. It also makes your house or flat seem larger. We simply took most of the junk to the local dump or to the charity shops. However, you could run a car boot sale. Or, if you have a lingering worry that you might just throw out something you need, put things in boxes dated several months or a year from now. Tuck the box out of the way in the loft or garage. Mark the date in your diary and, on that anniversary, throw the box away – preferably without looking inside.

Mark

When I first read about decluttering a few years ago, in Elaine St James's *Simplify Your Life*, I took it with a huge pinch of salt. How could I give up all those things that I had collected over the years? But I began gradually, clearing out the bathroom cabinet, the odd drawer and the garage (which seemed to be the repository of all the clutter that we had no space for in the house). Bit by bit, we moved around the room, house and shed. And slowly I realised the wisdom of her argument that decluttering can be 'a tremendously liberating experience'. We still have periodic purges.

Why new technology does not ease the 'housewife's burden'

Open any Sunday supplement or woman's magazine and you will be besieged by adverts for the latest time- and labour-saving devices. Sadly, many of these save neither time nor labour. Often they encourage a Mrs Parkinson's Law: housework expands to fill the time made available by the new labour-saving device.

Indeed, many studies now show that we spend as much time as our predecessors on the household chores. The reason is simple. Your grandmother used to have a washing day and her husband and children wore a shirt for two or three days – maybe even a week. Now we tend to change shirts every day, perhaps even a couple of times a day. So, while a washing machine means you can do the laundry more rapidly, there is more to do. The average British family now washes five loads a week. For some of us it is even more. As a result, we are using more energy, water and detergents than ever before, which increases damage to the environment.

Similarly, carpets used to be relatively rare: you picked up the rugs and beat them once a week. The floors could be brushed or mopped reasonably quickly. However, wall-to-wall carpets can take much longer to vacuum. And many people feel that they have to vacuum daily.

Finally, more women than ever now go to work. Yet, women still tend to do most of the housework. Sharing the chores with your partner and children or investing in a home help (see Chapter 9) may ease the burden. You could draw up a list of all the chores that need to be done and mark who is responsible. However, when you look at the list, ask yourself whether it is really necessary to vacuum every day? Is it really necessary to change a shirt each day? In addition, when you look to redecorate, consider low-maintenance decorations – such as floors you can quickly sweep rather than vacuum. We waste hours trying to be Mrs (or Mr) Beetons.

The new generation of techno-junkies

Modern technology has the potential to transform society: the way we work and the way we spend our leisure time. However, many of us are in danger of being burnt by the 'white heat of technology'. While the Internet offers us unprecedented access to information, it also has the potential to steal more and more of our time and money away from the things that we really want to do to help us realise our dreams.

We will soon be accessing the Internet through our digital televisions – but do we need 50 channels or the ability to pay bills during the commercial break? (The latter seems to engender a feeling that we should never take time off – there is always something to do.) Could we spend the time better elsewhere (remember the idea of opportunity costs)? And do not lose sight of the fact that these high-tech devices have an off switch.

However, when it comes to the Internet, we are in danger of breeding a generation of techno-junkies. While more and more of us now cruise the Information Superhighway, many of us cannot find the exit lane. Indeed, some users face an Internet addiction as serious as that experienced by gamblers, drugs abusers or alcoholics. This is not a rare problem facing a few computer 'nerds' – online surveys suggest that between 5 and 10 per cent of people using the Internet are addicts. So there may be a possibility that your teenager – or even you – could be at risk.

Apart from wasting time, Internet addiction can cause marital strife, failure in school or at work, debt and social isolation. A study from the University of Florida, released in 2000, found that, on average, addicts spent around 30 hours per week online *outside work* compared to three hours a week in work-related Internet activities. Many of these people suffer from so-called impulse control disorders (see page 41). They suffer growing anxiety about a behaviour that dissipates only when they are engaged in that behaviour.

If this sounds like you, you should probably seek psychiatric help (talk to your GP). However, many more people are now computer-chair potatoes, surfing the Internet in the same way they used to surf television channels. Keep an eye on how much you use the Internet. (Look at your phone bills or online clock.) Again, this brings up the idea of opportunity costs – by excessively using the Internet, you or your children are forgoing the opportunity to spend that time and money doing something else instead.

Are you a good role model?

Finally, remember that you are a role model for your children. As the self-help guru Richard Carlson notes, you should ask yourself what messages you are sending to your children. Are you calm and collected? Do you manage to cope with pressure? Are you organised? Remember, your behaviour influences your children's coping strategies.

In the same way, your parents were your role models for good or bad. As a result, if we want to be good role models for time and life management, we may need to reconsider and question many of the assumptions we grew up with, such as role divisions for men and women. Today, men tend to want to spend more time with their families, while women want satisfying careers. If, for example, your father was a distant figure who never played with his children and was always in the office, it does not mean that you have to be as well.

Chapter 9

Fifty ways to simplify your life

If time and life management aims to achieve one thing it is to make your life simpler; to stop you wasting your life on complexities that do not really matter. The time and life management techniques and tricks throughout this book should help you achieve this aim. However, this chapter rounds up 50 practical suggestions to help you achieve order. (You can find many other tips in the books and web sites in the Bibliography and Addresses section.) Not all of these will suit or apply to you. Nevertheless, these tips should help free your resources (temporal, spiritual and financial) to help you move towards your life goal, which is what time and life management is really all about.

Financial management

Looking after your financial health is one of the cornerstones of time and life management. We work, at least in part, to meet the first few steps on Maslow's hierarchy of needs (see page 67). However, many of us become trapped in a materialistic spiral, in which we have to keep up with the Joneses or feel compelled to surround ourselves with the trappings of success. This means, of course, that we need to work ever harder in our jobs. So we have less time at home or with our families and feel more stressed.

Yet, ironically, one of the 10 commandments to help us survive and thrive in the changing world (see Chapter 1) is to minimise our dependency on organisations, which may mean living well within our means. As a result, you will be better able to cope with unforeseen events that might threaten your income because you are used to living frugally. And look at it in a positive light: if you are financially less dependent on your employer, you have more options should you decide to set up your own business. Be honest: if you or your partner were suddenly laid off work tomorrow, would you be able to maintain your current standard of living? For how long would you even be able to continue payments on your home, car and credit cards?

Against this background, consider implementing some of the financial tips below. If you are interested in taking financial planning further, several books can help, including *The Which? Guide to Money* and *Be Your Own Financial Adviser* (Which? Books).

(1) Leave your credit cards at home

As anyone who has visited the United States knows, it is difficult to survive without 'charging'. However, in the UK many people find they can live without a credit card. Not having a credit card may mean that you are less likely to be tempted to buy on impulse items that you cannot really afford.

On the other hand, the disciplined use of a credit card – you have one card, with which you pay bills off in full every month – can be a useful budgeting tool and may simplify life. For example, you can have one transaction on your bank account statement each month rather than lots of little ones. Credit cards also offer a secure way of paying for items, provide added protection if things go wrong (with purchases over £100) and make e-commerce easier (although you can sometimes use debit cards on UK web sites). But you need to be disciplined. Certainly, if you pay off the balance each month, a credit card can be convenient, but paying interest on transactions makes life both chaotic and expensive.

If you are worried about the way you use credit cards, try leaving the card at home for a couple of months and see whether you save any money. If you are one of the people who pay interest, then consider cutting the card up – at least until you pay off your current debt. If you have a number of credit cards, begin with most expensive (generally shop cards) until you are left with one (preferably with a low interest rate). Having lots of small debts on many different cards can mask the fact that you might be in serious debt. Consolidating the debts on one low-interest card is cheaper – and may be chastening. If this is too much of a change, try carrying a smaller wallet. Leave some credit and charge cards at home. Then leave them all at home. Then get rid of them. However, remember that you can still run up considerable debts using debit cards and cash. It is more important to change your attitude to spending than to blame the payment method.

(2) Consider paying with cash alone

In many ways, charging is too easy, even if it directly debits your accounts. It is much harder handing over cash. Try this experiment. Pay with cash alone for a couple of weeks. This may illustrate, beyond reasonable doubt, how much you spend. Paying with cash alone, you can begin to establish a habit of considering the opportunity cost (see Chapter 1) of what you spend. The aim is to make you think about your spending habits, rather than to encourage you to pay with cash all the time. Do not carry too much in cash around with you, in case it gets stolen, and remember that you may need to pay charges if you need to use another bank's machine. Keep a note of what you spend the cash on. At least credit and debit card receipts give a clear record of your expenditure. Once you have made the point to yourself, try limiting yourself to a fixed cash sum each week – a budget helps you think twice about a purchase.

(3) Know what you spend

It is remarkable how few of us know where our hard-earned money goes. Indeed, according to a 1997 survey by a bank, half of those interviewed did not even know their current mortgage payment. A third did not know when they would finally pay off their mortgage.

To gain control of your financial situation, you could keep a diary of how much you spend and on what. This should include everything from the newspaper and cappuccino in the morning to the larger consumer items. Then look at your bank statements to see what you spend on direct debit. Keeping a diary of what you spend can be sobering and, rather like the time audits (pages 87–9), takes considerable discipline. Nevertheless, it is a very effective way of tracking your finances, especially over the short term, when you change your spending habits.

Alternatively, start with your known spending, which is shown on your bank statements and credit card statements. If this shows that your unknown spending is largely in cash, change to a payment method that leaves an audit trail and set a limit for cash spending.

Whichever approach you choose, try not to become too despond-ent about your position. Look at it positively. At least you are taking the first step in controlling your money.

(4) Develop a budget

Look at your daily and weekly spending after keeping a money diary for a couple of months and ask yourself if you are happy about how your money has been spent. Look at the direct debits and see if you can cut back (see point 7). Break your budget into essential spending (things you genuinely have to spend money on) and desirable purchases you do not strictly need. Consider reducing your essential spending by changing your mortgage lender, switching insurers or gas supplier and so on.

Based on this, you can develop a budget that allows you to live within your means and save for the future. On the food budget, for example, you might find you can reduce your expenditure by 25 per cent without too much difficulty, especially if you cook in bulk, take a packed lunch to work and entertain at home (see below). You may be able to shave even more off your personal expenditure. Develop-ing a budget allows you to spend as much of your income as possible on the things that matter to you.

(5) Know how much you have in your account

As part of this increased control, you should keep an eye on your account. Especially if you are making changes to the way that you spend, it is probably worth checking your account more regularly than a monthly statement allows. Fortunately, this is easy now with Internet, phone banking and statements from cash points. Remem-ber, however, that phone and Internet banking can push up your phone bills. You could switch to an Internet service provider (ISP) that offers free Internet access or reduced call charges to save money.

Regularly looking at your balance should help you avoid going overdrawn (or at least limit the size of the debt). But bear in mind that the balance may not be the same as the amount available to spend. Cheques still need a few days to clear, although they may appear on your statement before you can access the money. So it is important to keep a running balance and cross-check it regularly with your bank statement. Indeed, if you keep an accurate running balance you will soon gain the confidence to stop checking the state of your account.

(6) How much are you worth?

It is also worth keeping an eye on any stocks, shares, ISAs and PEPs you may have. For example, comparing interest rates means you can switch if you spot a better deal. However, with stocks, shares and ISAs you need to take a long-term view and not be too worried by short-term fluctuations in the stock market. For more information, see *The Which? Guide to Money* and *The Which? Guide to Shares* (Which? Books). *Be Your Own Financial Adviser*, also from Which? Books, explains how to organise your finances effectively and choose appropriate investments.

(7) Question your direct debits and regular bills

Paying regular bills by direct debit saves time and money: you do not need to write cheques for regular payments and many companies allow a discount for people paying this way. The problem is that it is all too easy to forget about the items you pay for by direct debit. Therefore, you need to review your direct debits and regular bills every so often to ensure that you are not paying over the odds for insurance and so on. For example:

- Do you still read the magazines you pay for each year?
- Do you still benefit from being a member of the organisations you belong to?
- Are you paying too much on your house or home insurance?
- What about the phone bill – can you cut it down (see point 14 below)?
- Do you really need critical illness, medical insurance *and* accident insurance?

You should question each item that you pay on direct debit and shop around for the best deal. Again, it is the uncontrolled spending habits that you need to address rather than the payment method. Reviewing your direct debits and regular bills helps you control your spending. It is worth blocking time off in your diary for this. *The Which? Guide to Insurance* (Which? Books) can help you decide what types of insurance are right for you.

(8) Consider consolidating your debts

If you cannot pay them off within a reasonable time, consider pooling your debts into one relatively low-interest loan. Shop around for the best interest rate. A wide variety is now available, especially over the Internet. But this works only if you close your other accounts. Remember that overdrafts, if approved in advance, may be cheaper than credit cards or many other loans. On the other hand, overdrafts can be more expensive due to the monthly fees charged. Moreover, overdrafts are repayable on demand. So they may not be suitable if you need time to pay off your debts. Again, the key is to shop around for the best deal that suits you.

(9) Pay back your debts in order of importance

If you are seriously in debt, you should pay your debts in order of importance. For most people, that means the mortgage or rent first; followed by gas, electricity and council tax; then your loans, credit cards and overdrafts. It is essential, if you know that you are beginning to slip into problems, to contact your creditors as soon as possible. This will probably buy you some time, and you may be able to reschedule your payments. Your local Citizens Advice Bureau and the National Debtline★ offer free debt counselling and may contact creditors on your behalf.

(10) Look after the pennies

This somewhat homely piece of advice is a valuable way, none the less, to help you control your spending. *It does not mean ignoring the big picture.* You need to ensure that you have sorted out the major issues affecting your current (and future) financial wellbeing first. Once you have done this, looking at the small items allows you to make choices between competing demands on your budget.

For instance, a supermarket sandwich, pub lunch or even a cup of coffee on the way to work may not seem like much, but the cost soon adds up into pounds. For example, you could eat a packed lunch rather than visiting the local sandwich bar and see how much you save over a month. A simple packed lunch may cost you £1 compared to perhaps £3 from a supermarket. That is a saving of £2 a day. Assuming you work 46 weeks per year, that is £460 a year. How many days do you need to work just to pay for your lunch?

You could also cut back on other minor areas – the money soon adds up. For example:

- a car wash costs several pounds. You will probably get a better result – and help your exercise requirement – by washing your own car
- turn the thermostat down by 1 degree centigrade. You probably will not notice the difference, but you could cut 10 per cent from your heating bill
- thinking about how much you spend on alcohol and cigarettes can be sobering – as well as giving you, if you need it, another good reason to quit smoking or control your drinking
- you could also try mixing-and-matching existing clothes rather than buying new outfits. Again, once you know how much you spend on clothes and the other small expenses using the diary (see point 3) you can see how much this saves.

Remember that while looking after the pennies can help free a few pounds and help you control your spending, you should always keep your eye on the big picture. Looking after the pennies adds detail to the big picture. It is not enough on its own.

(11) Do not believe the hype

During the 1950s, the economist John Galbraith revolutionised the way people considered modern society. His book *The Affluent Society*, which is still in print, laid bare the fact that, while society values work and productivity, many of the goods produced by this industrial drive are superfluous and serve only 'artificial' needs generated by high-pressure advertising. Indeed, he argues that the Western economic system is geared to cultivating and creating a demand for products through advertising and salesmanship that it can then meet. And, in many cases, these are fashionable and frivolous.

Moreover, Galbraith stressed that these 'created wants' generate debt. Indeed, demand depends on the 'ability and willingness of consumers to incur debt'. This underlines a point made several times throughout this book: advertising and society's expectations drive demand for consumer goods that add little to our lives, yet we are increasingly prepared to fall into debt to pay for such goods. We now see consumption *per se* as determining 'happiness', and buying consumer goods and services has become an end in itself.

This means that you need to question everything from advertising claims to the social norms. If you still feel that consumption meets your needs, fine. Most people want to wear reasonably fashionable clothes, for example. But is it worth changing your entire wardrobe each season, funded by your credit card? It is also useful to obtain independent evaluations, of expensive consumer goods and services, from organisations such as the Consumers' Association.* In other words: do not believe the hype. If you decide to buy the goods, fine − it is a conscious, deliberate decision. If not, you have saved your money and your time.

(12) Do not pay too much tax
Ensure that you take all the tax subsidies you are entitled to (see *The Which? Guide to Money* and *Which? Way to Save Tax* for more information − both from Which? Books). You may not need to employ an accountant: you can get help and advice for free from the Inland Revenue.*

(13) Understand why you shop
As we saw in Chapter 2, people who are close to becoming shopaholics often spend to relieve a feeling of anxiety. Few of us go this far but, nevertheless, many of us indulge to some degree in retail therapy. Tracking your expenses against your mood helps reveal this pattern. You are then better placed to do something about it. Trying some relaxation and meditation techniques (see Chapter 5 and points 39 and 40) may help.

(14) Do you really need 'call waiting' and other telephonic embellishments?
The phone bill is often a major expense as well as a source of arguments in families. So ask everyone to keep an eye on the phone calls. However, you can also cut your phone bill by dropping features such as 'call waiting', recall on engaged tones, answer services and so on. You could also consider changing your provider. In addition, you should keep any discount schemes up-to-date.

(15) Organise your paperwork
Be honest − if the Inland Revenue called, could you lay your hands on the paperwork to support your last return? Could you find the

instruction manual for the Hoover or microwave? If the answer is 'no', then you need to sort out your paperwork. You can use the paperwork suggestions in Chapter 7. Keep files for personal papers, such as: financial statements; pensions; credit cards; life insurance; proofs of purchase, warranties and guarantees; and so on. Remember, if you could not produce paperwork for the Inland Revenue you could face a fine for failing to keep proper records.

Some people go too far the other way and keep every credit card statement for the last 15 years, even for store cards that they no longer own. If this sounds like you, ask yourself whether you are likely to need this again. If it is for tax reasons, you need to keep the document. However, there may be a lot of paperwork that you can bin.

(16) Go high-tech

If you are comfortable using the Internet, online banking, with its 24-hour service and competitive rates, is worth considering. In addition, as noted above, the high-tech accounts mean that it is easier to keep track of your current balance. Digital televisions offer access to bank accounts, so you can even manage your finances during commercial breaks. There is even a microwave oven that allows you to check your balance and pay bills while warming your food. (But if you need such a device, perhaps you would do better to slow down instead.)

Modern computerised banking also allows you to use automated transactions, which can be especially useful if you cannot get to your local branch. Some people even transfer their children's allowances into their accounts automatically. However, handing out pocket money is a family ritual (see Chapter 8), and you should think hard before automating this transaction.

You can also use automated standing orders to put any spare money into high-interest accounts, but just as with the direct debits, it is worth keeping a regular check on just how much is being automatically debited from your account. Also, remember that phone and Internet banking can push up your phone bills. Keeping an accurate running balance (see point 5) can instil the confidence you need to stop checking the state of your account.

Using a computer spreadsheet to do your budgeting saves time and can help to take the tedium out of adding up columns of figures.

(17) Save for a rainy day

Today, few people have significant savings, but rely on their job for economic security. As a result, most of us live in an environment dominated by insecurity. Therefore, it makes sense to try to weave yourself an economic safety net. In other words, try to live within your means – and, if you are lucky enough to come into a windfall, do not spend all of it at once. Save some for a rainy day. Saving up for something specific can also help you impose some discipline on your spending.

One way to do this is to write yourself a cheque for, say, 5 or 10 per cent of your income every payday. Put this aside in a high-interest account or ISA. Provided that you are not struggling to repay your mortgage and the bailiffs are not knocking on the door, you will probably find there is still enough for the bills. Of course, you will need to make choices – opportunity costs are at issue again. However, this nest egg will grow gradually.

Another approach is to wait until your next promotion and put at least half the increase aside (again, into a high-interest account or ISA). Indeed, not raising your standard of living just because you have got a promotion or moved to a better-paid job can help you control your expenditure. Many financial consultants suggest that you should have about three to six months' expenses put aside. While this may take several years to build up, it offers a degree of financial security in an uncertain world.

(18) Think about home help

As time becomes ever more stretched, many of us employ home helps. It is a sign of our time-pressurised lifestyles that the demand for such services is huge. About four million people work in domestic service, making it the fastest-growing sector of the economy. Indeed, Britain now has more cleaners, gardeners and nannies than accountants.

For people facing numerous demands, home help certainly allows them to buy back their time. However, hiring home help can be expensive. So, you need to weigh up the cost against the benefit of hiring someone to do the housework. Perhaps, if you work for yourself, you may decide you would rather do the domestic chores yourself. On the other hand, you can make a trade-off between the cost of employing someone else and maybe sharing the chores around the family. For information on hiring help in the home, see *The Which? Guide to Domestic Help* (Which? Books).

(19) Budget for Christmas and holidays

Ideally, you should save up for birthdays, Christmas and holidays. Then you can set yourself a budget and stick to it. This should limit the amount you need to charge to your credit card or your overdraught.

(20) Wait before you buy something

One key to financial success is to ask yourself how much you really need, or want, something before you buy it. How long will you use or wear it? How many times will you read the book or play the CD? If possible, do not buy the item immediately. Wait a few days and see if you still feel that it is useful or beautiful enough to warrant the hours that you have spent working in order to pay for it.

(21) Make lists of 'needs', 'wants' and 'luxuries'

These speak for themselves, but the challenge lies in deciding which is which. Do you really need that new coat or pair of shoes? Is that new laptop really a luxury, or is it something you want because it will increase your business productivity and save you time? Is there a cheaper alternative for something on your luxury list? Again, this should help you spend only on those items that really enhance your quality of life. It is also worth thinking about the ethical, environmental and social issues behind many products and services. *Ethical Consumer*★ magazine examines these in depth.

(22) Take the time to manage your money

As various people have observed, there are probably more money-making opportunities today than ever before. These money-making opportunities range from share-dealing to home businesses to running your own web site. The writer Richard Carlson suggests spending an hour each day investigating strategies and business opportunities to help you towards financial independence.

While many of us may not want to become involved to this extent, it is well worth taking the time to manage money effectively. In a recent building society survey, a third of the families questioned admitted failing to manage their money properly because they had insufficient time. Depending on how complex – or messy – your finances are, it might be worth putting aside an hour a week or so to go through your income and outgoings. You can use this time to check statements (banks make mistakes), keep track of investments, ensure that you are staying on budget, examine direct debits and so on. You might not need as long as an hour, but if you have set the time aside you will find that the routine helps put you in control of your finances.

Family life

One of the foremost reasons why people want to manage their time more efficiently is to spend longer with their families. Certainly, many people find themselves under so much time pressure that they are unable to cope with the daily chores, let alone spend quality time with the children. In a recent survey, two-thirds of the people with children could not cope with housework and 56 per cent could not find the time for a supermarket shop, for example. However, you can also take several steps to make your life at home a little more straightforward. For example:

(23) Prepare for the next day the night before
Prepare for the whole family's departure (to school, work and so on) the night before. Put coats, briefcases and bags by the door, and ensure that they are packed with everything you and your children need. Also, agree on one place to keep the car keys.

(24) Keep a money pot
Put your loose change into a pot in the hall or kitchen. That way you will not waste time finding change for charity, the bus or for parking.

(25) Keep 'emergency' numbers close to hand
Pin the numbers you use the most – such as pizza delivery (if you do not cook in bulk), as well as important numbers, such as the doctor's, the dentist's and a neighbour's – on to a pin board by the phone or in the kitchen. And let your children know where they are in case of emergency. You could also program the memory buttons on your phone with some of these.

(26) Journey times

Add between five and 30 minutes, depending on distance, to every journey you plan to make. This allows for last-minute delays before you leave the house, problems on the road and so on. As a result, you should arrive at most of your appointments on time, fluster-free and without a speeding ticket.

(27) Do your chores together

Try also to think about your weekly tasks. Are there any trips you can combine? Can you go to the bank at the same time as the supermarket? Can you collect your dry-cleaning when taking your daughter to Brownies, for instance? Your time audit should help identify chores you can do in batches.

(28) Share the chores

In 1999, the Future Foundation reported that men have an average of 40 hours' leisure time a week. Women have an average of just 13.5 hours. Clearly, then, partners could aim to share the non-workday tasks – housework, DIY and so on. One way would be for both partners to log the time spent on commitments at home to see how the tasks can be shared more equally. And do not forget the children: they may also be able to take some of the chores off your hands – even if it means a rise in their allowance.

(29) Declutter family leisure time

If you want to try something new, what will you give up? You probably do not have the time to do everything. The idea of opportunity costs applies here too – taking up a new hobby may mean spending less time on the sofa. However, it may also mean giving up something else. The same applies to your children. If they want to join a new club or learn something new, ensure they have enough time to do it properly. Otherwise, ask them to give up something to create time. Asking them to choose also helps you to determine whether this will be a 'flash in the pan' or something that they really want to do.

(30) Declutter together

When your children buy a new toy or game, encourage them to get rid of something else. You can also spend some time going through their rooms and getting rid of the toys they never play with, the games they have grown out of and the inevitable jigsaw with missing pieces. It makes keeping their rooms tidy easier and helps them find the space for their hobbies. Similarly, most families have boxes of photos they never look at. Sort them out together. Throw out the out-of-focus photos and those that make you cringe. Keep the ones you like and put them in albums. You can give the others away or let your children use them to make collages or cards.

(31) Take time for yourself

However engrossed you might be with family or other commitments, you need to ensure that you get some time for yourself at the end of each day, even if it is just half an hour. Read a book, listen to some music, have a bath – whatever it takes to relax. Taking time for yourself also allows you to reflect on the day or write a diary entry (see point 47). Both activities can help you track your progress towards your ultimate goal, as well as ensure that your choices fit in with your personal values.

(32) The family that gardens together . . .

Gardening is a sure-fire stress-buster: it helps you reach your exercise requirement and, as you see plants grow, gives an immense feeling of satisfaction. Children of all ages also love growing flowers and vegetables. Gardening can be a true bonding experience.

(33) Eat in sometimes

Eating out with friends can be expensive – and organising childcare, if needed, can be a logistical nightmare. Eating in with friends can be a much less expensive alternative. This does not mean holding formal dinner parties, but simply asking everyone to bring some food along and hold a buffet or a barbecue.

(34) Think about how you shop

Supermarkets are supposed to exist for our convenience. Yet we spend about 90 minutes a week in the supermarket, the same as 20 years ago. The difference is that today, instead of a single journey each week, we make an average of three shorter trips. However, many people cannot even find the time to do this. Sixty per cent of families in a recent building society survey said they resorted to shopping at more expensive convenience shops as they could not find time to visit a supermarket. You might find it worthwhile to note in your diary your weekly visits to the supermarket; then see if you can consolidate these trips. Keep a list of the supplies you need regularly – perhaps on computer, so you can print it out easily. In some cases, you may be able to join together with friends and shop in bulk. The savings can be considerable.

(35) Try cooking in bulk

As our time comes under increasing pressure, our diets are among the first casualties. And our health may suffer as a direct result: processed foods are usually high in, for example, saturated fat and salt, both of which we should limit. However, making a meal after a day at work may seem like hard work. The answer may be to use the freezer and cook in batches. Just make double the quantity you would normally and freeze half. You can reheat the frozen portion when you are pushed for time. However, try to have several 'slower' meals a week.

Some people say that it is possible to cook a month's worth of meals and store them in the freezer. Certainly, most people should be able to store a few days' worth of food. Cooking in bulk helps avoid the problem of having to rely on fast food during the week, which can save considerable amounts of money – a recent survey found that the average family spends around £20 a week on takeaways. Frozen Assets* offers advice on how to 'Cook for a Day and Eat for a Month'.

(36) Accept that you are not Mrs (or Mr) Beeton

Many people seem to want to be perfect homekeepers, as well as a success in their career and in their personal life. Of course, this is difficult, if not impossible. There simply are not enough hours in the day to do everything to perfection. You need to decide what is important to you (see Chapter 1, opportunity costs). How important is it to have an immaculate house, rather than one that is neat most of the time and sanitary all the time? Accept a few toys lying around or an unmade bed. Mess really depends on how you look at it. Toys sprinkled around the living room are a sign that your children play a central point in your life.

(37) Decide whether you really need a home help

As we noted under point 18 above, a home help *may* be one of the few ways you can free up valuable time. Some people would be unable to find any time for themselves without relying on domestic services. However, home help is a drain on most family's budgets. So think carefully and balance the costs against the time you will gain before you take the plunge. You can use the idea of opportunity costs to decide whether it is worth spending money on a home help.

(38) Keep things together

Keep your shoes in one place. (Anyone who has spent 20 minutes trying to find a toddler's shoe only for it to turn up in the most improbable place knows how much time this could save.) Keep your kitchen utensils and tools grouped together. Put things that you do not use often in a labelled box. When you plan to redecorate, plan your storage space to allow you to keep things together.

Spirituality

Today, most of our lives seem focused on the external world – our jobs and possessions, for example. However, nurturing our spiritual side helps bolster our defences against stress and also awakens us to a wider reality. However, you need to be committed to developing this side of your life.

Nurturing your spiritual side is part of the balance that time and life management helps you develop. Indeed, unless you make the effort to free time elsewhere, these efforts will fall by the wayside. As David Fontana points out in *The Meditator's Handbook*, meditation needs to become part of our daily lives, both in terms of practising regularly and in terms of the importance that we attach to it. Fontana argues that meditation, whichever form it takes, prevents our real nature from becoming hidden by the demands made on us by work, family life and the wider social culture.

Which form of meditation you choose is down to you. However, they all help you get in touch with a deeper reality and keep your problems in perspective. Your life will be richer as a result. Indeed, as Thoreau wrote: 'Most men, even in this comparatively free country . . . are so occupied with the factitious cares and superfluously coarse labours of life that its finer fruits cannot be plucked by them.'

Developing your inner side keeps these 'factitious cares and superflu-ously coarse labours' in context and is one of the richest of these finer fruits.

(39) Consider taking up t'ai chi

T'ai chi and yoga (see point 40) aim to integrate your mind and body. While both can look simple – some of the more extreme yoga positions apart – they are mentally, physically and spiritually demand-ing. For example, various forms of t'ai chi involve 100 positions, and to gain the most from yoga you should follow a number of rules about lifestyle.

Both these forms of exercise highlight the fact that our bodies are unruly and difficult to control. In addition, both disciplines are spiritually demanding because both are forms of meditation, with their roots deep in eastern philosophy.

You can follow one of a number of t'ai chi schools that differ in their styles. Moreover, within each school, each teacher may bring his or her own interpretations to the form. For example, some may concentrate on the martial side, while others emphasise the spiritual. Nevertheless, all the schools integrate meditation, self-defence and healing. (There is some evidence that t'ai chi can alleviate a number of stress-related illnesses and help relieve conditions such as arthritis.) A number of books and videos can give you a feel for t'ai chi, but you will need instruction from a teacher to participate. Contact the National T'ai Chi Chaun Association★ and the British Council of Chinese Martial Arts.★

(40) Consider taking up yoga

Millions of people worldwide find that yoga brings them a sense of inner peace and relief from stress, as well as improved health and general sense of wellbeing. Yoga helps keep your mind and body supple, relaxed and strong. It offers a complete physical, mental and spiritual system to help you balance your life. Yoga practitioners see the physical, mental and spiritual aspects as intertwined. Indeed, the Indian root of the word 'yoga' means to unite, with the aim of stilling the mind's restless movement. As such, it helps free us from the concerns and fears that can sometimes plague us.

For example, the yoga postures – *asanas* – are more than stretching exercises. Correctly performed, asanas involve mental control, correct breathing and using the body efficiently and effectively. As asanas gently stretch and contract muscles and joints, they help you move more freely and improve your stamina, flexibility and strength. They also take considerable concentration and train the mind to focus on the present, raising one's consciousness. In addition, as correct breathing is essential, you feel more energised. Indeed – as with most forms of meditation that also focus on breathing – yoga helps you control your mental and physical processes. For example, many people with asthma and depression find that yoga helps, although they should continue to take any drugs prescribed by a doctor.

Once again, you can gain an impression of yoga from a wide range of books and videos, but you will need to attend classes and practice for 20–30 minutes each day to benefit. Contact the British Wheel of Yoga★ and the Yoga for Health Foundation.★ Your library or adult education centres may also have details of local courses.

(41) Read something inspirational each day
This could be a religious or philosophical book, a collection of quotations or poetry, or a more modern book – perhaps the work of a self-help author such as Richard Carlson or Elaine St James. Consider the reading during the day and see whether it helps you to see problems in a new light.

(42) Read biographies
Reading about the life and times, and maybe the trials and tribulations, of other people often helps with your own life. Biographies can also be inspirational and help motivate you along your path to self-fulfilment.

(43) Read something about which you know nothing
Many of us read the same paper for years. We watch the same programmes on television, listen to the same music, visit the same places, read books about the same topics. However, confronting something totally new keeps you mentally alert. It may open a completely new world to you, which will enhance your creativity.

(44) Spend some time in the countryside or by the sea
Sometimes the best thing we can do is to get away from it all. Spending some time in the natural world, away from the 'madding

crowd', allows us to keep our worries and concerns in perspective. Enjoy the moment: watch the sunset or admire the flora and fauna. It is a valuable way to recharge your mental and physical batteries, and you will probably perform much more effectively once you return.

(45) Do not rely on your holiday being the answer to stress

Many television advertisements and programmes, as well as lifestyle and travel features in magazines and newspapers, seem to suggest that holidays are the antidote to stress. Do not assume that your holiday will get rid of your stress. A mid-1990s Gallup poll found that 53 per cent of those questioned said taking a holiday was for them the most stressful life event over the last year.

Rather than relying on a single holiday, it is perhaps better to rediscover some of the simple pleasures during regular short breaks throughout the year, either at home or elsewhere. These can act as first aid for stress, preventing worries from becoming too much to bear. They also help you develop your family relationships and make the most of all that time you have freed up using the techniques outlined in this book.

(46) Nurture your creativity

As suggested earlier in the book, creativity is to an ever-growing extent the key to success at work, and in life as a whole. However, being creative can also help you stay in touch with your inner self, as well as offer a great way to unwind. What you do does not matter. As the psychologist Abraham Maslow pointed out, you can be creative in cooking and home-making just as much as in poetry and painting. Attending an evening course in something that appeals can help you unleash your creative potential. Moreover, nurturing your creativity in one area often spills over into another. So, if you take up a creative hobby, you may well find yourself being more creative at work and at home.

(47) Keep a journal

Historians would be lost without the journals and diaries kept by our predecessors. More prosaically, keeping a journal is one way to tackle the tasks outlined in Chapter 4. It also acts as a record of the problems you have faced and helps you see just how far you have come.

Finally, keeping a journal also allows you to try therapeutic writing. You can express your innermost thoughts and dreams as well as put yourself in touch with your creative side.

(48) Slow down

Often it seems almost obligatory to rush around. But forcing yourself to slow down enables you to appreciate the subtleties of life. As the writer Elaine St James points out, slowing down helps you stay in touch with how you are feeling and what you are doing. It also makes it possible to explore and enjoy each moment. For example, try walking instead of taking the car and see what is around you; and try eating more slowly, really concentrating on the flavours of different foods.

(49) Do not let little things get you down

The American writer Richard Carlson wrote several books focusing on and developing this simple advice – and with good reason. Its simplicity hides its profundity. All of us, at one time or another, become anxious and angry about things that, in the final analysis, do not really matter. Whether it is waiting in the bank, being cut up on the road or having a row with a co-worker or spouse, we are adept at building mountains from molehills. But by 'not sweating the small stuff' – by not allowing the small things to take over from what really matters – we will stay on track with our larger plans, be less stressed and make better use of our time. Few things waste as much time as unnecessary worrying.

(50) Use your imagination

These ideas are only suggestions. Your life is unique and precious. Once you know and understand your values and philosophy, once you know your life destination, you should be able to find many more ways to simplify your life, which will free your time and resources for the things that really matter.

Chapter 10

Putting it all together

This chapter draws together some themes outlined in the rest of the book and summarises the main messages. Many conventional time and life management books explore the ways in which people can maximise their productivity at work and at home, but ignore Parkinson's Law: a job will expand to fill the available time. You may be more effective, but your in-tray will never be empty. Also, there is a growing recognition among commentators, from downshifters living in wood cabins to leading management consultants, of the benefits of restoring a sense of balance in our lives – personally, as well as in terms of our families and work. Indeed, surviving and thriving in a changing world means looking beyond time management to life management, which Lennart Meynert defines as 'a system designed to give you control over your life'.

Take a broad view

If there is one central message in this book, it is that to be truly effective and efficient we need to look at the broader picture rather than simply at the home or work environment. Remember the crucial difference between being effective and being efficient: if you are efficient, you perform the task correctly – the essence of time management; if you are effective, you perform the correct task – the essence of life management. Conventional time management focuses on making you efficient, but ignores whether you are effective in your life overall. Life management allows you to look at the broader picture.

So, for example, time and life management means considering your finances. Many of us become trapped in a materialistic spiral, in which we feel compelled to surround ourselves with the trappings of success. This means, of course, that we need to work ever harder in our jobs. So we have less time and we feel more stressed. Ironically, one of the 10 commandments to help us survive and thrive in the changing world (summarised below) is to minimise our dependency on organisations. That means living within our means. Then, if the worst happens, we have a safety net. If you are financially less dependent on your employer, you have more options.

Managing your life also means nurturing your spiritual side. Nurturing spirituality helps bolster our defences against stress; it can also awaken us to a wider reality. However, you need to be committed to develop this side of your life, just as much as you need to be committed to life-long learning at work and making the most of time spent with your family.

It is also important to keep work in perspective. We may spend more hours at work than at home, but it should not dominate our lives. There is a price (opportunity cost) to pay for spending more time at work – your health, family relationships, social and leisure time can all suffer. Working long hours is not even good news for your employer, as it can compromise morale and productivity. So, question the assumption that you have to work harder. Instead, work smarter using the time and life management techniques.

Certainly, if you manage your time you are better able to manage your life, and the ability to do this will matter even more as the pace of change quickens. Companies transform their size and structure more rapidly than ever before in response to evolving markets and there is a global trend towards mergers and buyouts. Today, no job is for life. Indeed, many people – including traditional professionals – no longer know if their job will still exist next year, next month or even next week.

These strategies can help you restore a sense of balance between work and family, as well as between your personal commitments and ambitions. They also help you to develop a sense of meaning in your lives, to create a personal philosophy and value set, and to identify a goal that you want to work towards. In other words, you need to impose control on your life while developing a vision of where you want to go and how you intend to get there.

Survive and thrive

The management researcher Trix Webber highlights several strategies to help us survive and thrive in a changing world. We can apply them to any or all aspects of our lives – and they all rely on efficient time and life management.

- Be absolutely committed to your learning and development
- Become a creative learner
- Envision the future
- Form support groups
- Marginalise your dependency on the organisation you work for
- Give loyalty appropriately
- Have realistic expectations of organisations
- Be politically aware
- Develop your negotiating capacity
- Plan your career intrapreneurially and entrepreneurially. (Remember that an intrapreneur is innovative within a company; an entrepreneur sets up a new company to develop the innovation.)

Take an exit from the road to nowhere

Once you have developed a sense of meaning and a vision of your destination, you can use the fundamentals of time and life management to build your road towards your ultimate aim. This book suggests how to develop a time and life management tool kit which you can use at home and at work to help you move more rapidly along this road. Indeed, it is essential not to confine time and life management to the office. The same techniques can increase the quality and quantity of time you spend with your family.

The ten essentials of time and life management

Ideas need to move from theory into practice. There is nothing wrong with making detailed plans, but eventually you need to act on them. As Thoreau noted: 'If you have built castles in the air, your work need not be lost; that is where they should be. Now put the foundations under them.' The ten essentials of time and life management allow you to lay these foundations.

(1) Develop a personal philosophy and value set along with a vision of where you want to go.

(2) Identify long-term goals that are in line with this philosophy and value set. Hitting these should take you towards your ultimate ambition.

(3) Identify short-term goals that are in line with this philosophy and value set, and that help you reach each long-term goal.

(4) Establish a balance between your work, family and personal commitments. Again, this should be in line with your personal philosophy and value set.

(5) Plan each day using a diary and a 'to do' list, either on paper or on computer.

(6) Decide your home and work priorities. Aim to spend 80 per cent of your time at home and at work on your priorities.

(7) Organise and simplify your life at home and at work. Living simply does not necessarily mean moving to a log cabin and living close to poverty. Rather, it means organising your life so that you do not waste your time on pointless activities that do not take you any closer to your ultimate aim.

(8) Manage your health as carefully as you manage your work.

(9) Be committed to life-long learning. However, take only what is useful and question any advice you are given to see what is appropriate for you. In time and life management, there are no sacred cows.

(10) Audit your progress at all levels, from the impact of small changes to the progress you are making towards your ultimate ambition as well as what you have learnt from the experience. After two years of living the 'good life', for example, Thoreau learnt that: 'If one advances confidently in the direction of his dreams, and endeavours to live the life which he has imagined, he will meet with a success unexpected in common hours.'

If there is a second take-home message, it is that you should you live deliberately. In *Walden,* as discussed in Chapter 1 of this book, Thoreau wrote about going to the woods 'because I wished to live deliberately, to front only the essential facts of life, and see if I could not learn what it had to teach, and not, when I came to die, discover that I had not lived. I wanted to live deep and suck out all the marrow of life.'

The key word is 'deliberately'. While moving in a rural idyll may sound tempting, few of us can – or would want to – live the 'good life'. But the philosophy of living deliberately and getting all you can from life can apply whether you live in a log cabin or in an executive home, whether you work collecting berries or in a boardroom. Everyone has to make choices. Those choices should be made deliberately. Making deliberate choices enriches your life. That is what time and life management is all about.

Bibliography

Some of these articles and books are mentioned in the text. This section also includes suggestions for further reading.

Introduction
Cooper, C.L. and Worrall, L. 1999. *The Quality of Working Life: 1999 Survey of Managers' Changing Experiences*. Institute of Management

Chapter 1 From the log cabin to the boardroom
Adair, J. 1999. *Time Management and Personal Development*. Hawksmere

Clegg, B. 2000. How to have time for your life. *Professional Manager*, Jan, 18–20

Cropley, M., Steptoe, A., Joekes, K. 1999. Job strain and psychiatric morbidity. *Psychol Med*, **29**, 1411–16

1999. Decide now. *Management Today*, July, 60–1

Greener, M.J. 1996. *The Which? Guide to Managing Stress*. Which? Books

Johnson, P.R. 1995. Brains, heart and courage: keys to empowerment and self-directed leadership. *American Journal of Management Development*, **1**, 16–21

Kakimoto, Y., Nakamura, A., Tarui, H. et al. 1988. Crew workload in JASDF C-1 transport flights: I. Change in heart rate and salivary cortisol. *Aviat Space Environ Med*, **59**, 511–16

Maslow, A.H. 1999. *Toward a Psychology of Being*. Wiley, 3rd edition

Meynert, L. 1989. *Life Management: live better by working smarter*. Oldcastle

Singer, I. 1996. *The Harmony of Nature and Spirit*. The Johns Hopkins University Press

Tempus – the Art of Time. 2000. Fitzwilliam Museum, Cambridge

Taylor, D., Edge, D. 1997. Personal development plans: unlocking the future. *Career Development International*, **2**, 21–3

Thoreau, H.D. *Walden and Other Writings*. 1993. Barnes & Noble Classics

Webber, T. 1997. Strategies for surviving and thriving in organisations. *Career Development International*, **2**, 90–2

Chapter 2 Why time and life management isn't just for yuppies

1997. Are You Stressed Out? *Family Practice Management*, March, 85

Burke, R.J., MacDermid, G. 1999. Are workaholics job satisfied and successful in their careers? *Career Development International*, **4**, 277–82

Cole, T.R. 1992. *The Journey of Life: A Cultural History of Aging in America*. Canto

Greener, M.J. 1996. *The Which? Guide to Managing Stress*. Which? Books

Hurley, A.E., Giannantonio, C.M. 1999. Career attainment for women and minorities: the interactive effects of age, gender and race. *Women in Management Review,* **14**, 4–13

Kenney, J.W. 2000. Women's 'inner-balance': a comparison of stressors, personality traits and health problems by age groups. *Journal of Advanced Nursing*, **31**, 639–50

Mavin, S. 2000. Approaches to careers in management: why UK organisations should consider gender. *Career Development International*, **5**, 13–20

Meynert, L. 1989. *Life Management: live better by working smarter*. Oldcastle

Scarnati, J. 1999. Beyond technical competence: the fundamentals of flexibility. *Participation & Empowerment: An International Journal*, **7**, 194–200

Scarnati, J.T. 1999. Beyond technical competence: the art of leadership. *Career Development International*, **4**, 325–35

Storr, A. 1972. *The Dynamics of Creation*. Penguin

Sturges, J. 1999. What it means to succeed: personal conceptions of career success held by male and female managers at different ages. *British Journal of Management*, **10**, 239–52

Chapter 3 Understanding change

Carlson, R. 1997. *Don't Sweat the Small Stuff*. Hyperion

Carlson, R. 1998. *Don't Sweat the Small Stuff with Your Family*. Hyperion

Maslow, A.H. 1999. *Toward a Psychology of Being*. Wiley, 3rd edition

Singer, I. 1996. *The Harmony of Nature and Spirit*. The Johns Hopkins University Press

Zimmerman, G.L., Olsen, C.G., Bosworth, M.F. 2000. A 'stages of change' approach to helping patients change behavior. *Am Fam Physician*, **61**, 1409–16

Meynert, L. 1989. *Life Management: live better by working smarter*. Oldcastle

Chapter 4 What really matters

Adair, J. 1999. *Time Management and Personal Development*. Hawksmere

Carlson, R. 1997. *Don't Sweat the Small Stuff*. Hyperion

Carlson, R. 1998. *Don't Sweat the Small Stuff with Your Family*. Hyperion

Clegg, B. 2000. How to have time for your life. *Professional Manager*, 18–20

Dancer, J. 2000. Vision to reality. *Pharmaceutical Times*, April, 46–7

Decide Now. 1999. *Management Today*, July, 60–1

Johnson, P.R. 1995. Brains, heart and courage: keys to empowerment and self-directed leadership. *American Journal of Management Development*, **1**, 16–21

Maslow, A.H. 1999. *Toward a Psychology of Being*, Wiley, 3rd edition

Meynert, L. 1989. *Life Management: live better by working smarter*. Oldcastle

Scarnati, J. 1999. Beyond technical competence: the fundamentals of flexibility. *Participation & Empowerment: An International Journal*, **7**, 194–200.

Scarnati, J.T. 1999. Beyond technical competence: the art of leadership. *Career Development International*, **4**, 325–35

Sturges, J. 1999. What it means to succeed: personal conceptions of career success held by male and female managers at different ages. *British Journal of Management*, **10**, 239–52

Taylor, D., Edge, D. 1997. Personal development plans: unlocking the future. *Career Development International*, **2**, 21–3

Thompson, M. 1994. *Ethics*. Teach Yourself Books

Chapter 5 The essential elements of time and life management

Baldwin, D. 1994. Social phobia – the abhorrence of scrutiny. *Psychiatry in Practice*, Winter, 4

Bolden, K. 1996. Transactional analysis. *Practice Nursing*, **7** (12), 4–8

Bruce, T.J. and Saeed, S.A. 1999. Social anxiety disorder: a common, underrecognized mental disorder. *Am Fam Physician*, **60**, 2311–22

Carducci, B. 2000. Shyness the new solution. *Psychology Today*, Jan/Feb, 39–45, 78

Greener, M.J. 1990. Addiction: GP advice a successful therapy. *MIMS magazine*, 15 June, 18

Greener, M.J. 1990. Where GP counselling can cut therapy costs. *MIMS magazine*, 1 Oct, 15

Hindle, T. 1998. *Manage Your Time*. Dorling Kindersley

Mayer, J.J. 1995. *Time Management for Dummies*. IDG Books

Meynert, L. 1989. *Life Management: live better by working smarter*. Oldcastle

Reynolds, H., Tramel, M.E. 1979. *Executive Time Management*. Prentice-Hall

St James, E. 1995. *Inner Simplicity*. Hyperion

St James, E. 1994. *Simplify Your Life*. Hyperion

Taylor, D., Edge, D. 1997. Personal development plans: unlocking the future. *Career Development International*, **2**, 21–3

Chapter 6 Increase your time

Bensing, J.M., Hulsman, R.L., Schreurs, K.M. 1999. Gender differences in fatigue: biopsychosocial factors relating to fatigue in men and women. *Med Care*, **37**, 1078–83

Bourbeau, J., Brisson, C., Allaire, S. 1996. Prevalence of the sick building syndrome symptoms in office workers before and after being exposed to a building with an improved ventilation system. *Occup Environ Med*, **53**, 204–10

de Rijk, A.E., Schreurs, K.M., Bensing, J.M. 1999. What is behind 'I'm so tired'? Fatigue experiences and their relations to the quality and quantity of external stimulation. *J Psychosom Res*, **47**, 509–23

Fontana, D. 1992. *The Meditator's Handbook*. Element

Iversen, S.D. 1986. *Psychopharmacology: recent advances and future prospects*. Oxford University Press

Kleiner, S.M. 1999. Water: an essential but overlooked nutrient. *J Am Diet Assoc*, **99**, 200–6

Koskinen, O.M., Husman, T.M., Meklin, T.M. et al. 1999. The relationship between moisture or mould observations in houses and the state of health of their occupants. *Eur Respir J*, **14**, 1363–7

Marsden, G. and Leach, J. 2000. Effects of alcohol and caffeine on maritime navigational skills. *Ergonomics*, **43**, 17–26

Martikainen, K., Partinen, M., Hasan, J. et al. 1998. Natural evolution of sleepiness. A 5-year follow-up study in a middle-aged population. *Eur J Neurol*, **5**, 355–63

Mendell, M.J., Fisk, W.J., Deddens, J.A., et al. 1996. Elevated symptom prevalence associated with ventilation type in office buildings. *Epidemiology*, **7**, 583–9

Robelin, M., Rogers, P.J. 1998. Mood and psychomotor performance effects of the first, but not of subsequent, cup-of-coffee equivalent doses of caffeine consumed after overnight caffeine abstinence. *Behav Pharmacol*, **9**, 611–18

van der Linden, G., Chalder, T., Hickie, I. et al. 1999. Fatigue and psychiatric disorder: different or the same? *Psychol Med*, **29**, 863–8

Watt, G.C., Britton, A., Gilmour, W.H. et al. 1996. Is lead in tap water still a public health problem? An observational study in Glasgow. *BMJ*; **313**, 979–81

1996. *Sleeptalking*, Summer, **1** (1), 1–8

Chapter 7 Time and life management at work

Crandall, R. (ed). 1998. *Break-out Creativity*. Select Press

Dobson, A. 1999. *Managing Meetings*. How To Books, 2nd edition

Gandham, S.R. 1994. Occupational Stress. *Psychiatry in Practice*, Winter, 10–12

Hindle, T. 1998. *Manage Your Time*. Dorling Kindersley

Kennard, C. 1996. *Managing Your Boss*. Gower

Lynn, M. 2000. How to manage your boss. *Management Today*, Jan, 66–8

Marler, P., Mattia, J.B. 1998. *Time Management Made Easy*. VGM Career Horizons

Mayer, J.J. 1995. *Time Management for Dummies*. IDG Books

Meynert, L. 1989. *Life Management: live better by working smarter*. Oldcastle

Reynolds, H., Tramel, M.E. 1979. *Executive Time Management*. Prentice-Hall

Storr, A. 1972. *The Dynamics of Creation*. Penguin Books

Webber, T. 1997. Strategies for surviving and thriving in organisations. *Career Development International*, **2**, 90–2

White, M. 1997. *Isaac Newton: the Last Sorcerer*. Fourth Estate

Chapter 8 Time and life management and your family

Carlson, R. 1998. *Don't Worry, Make Money*. Hodder & Stoughton

Carlson, R. 1997. *Don't Sweat the Small Stuff*. Hyperion

Carlson, R. 1998. *Don't Sweat the Small Stuff with Your Family*. Hyperion

Galbraith, J.K. 1991. *The Affluent Society*. Penguin, 4th edition

Levine, K. 1996. *Keeping Life Simple*. Storey

Luhrs, J. 1997. *The Simple Living Guide*. Broadway Books

Meynert, L. 1989. *Life Management: live better by working smarter*. Oldcastle

St James, E. 1995. *Inner Simplicity*. Hyperion

St James, E. 1994. *Simplify Your Life*. Hyperion

Chapter 9 *Fifty ways to simplify your life*
Carlson, R. 1998. *Don't Worry, Make Money*. Hodder & Stoughton
Carlson, R. 1997. *Don't Sweat the Small Stuff*. Hyperion
Carlson, R. 1998. *Don't Sweat the Small Stuff with Your Family*. Hyperion
Fontana, D. 1992. *The Meditator's Handbook*. Element
Galbraith, J.K. 1991. *The Affluent Society*. Penguin, 4th edition
Levine, K. 1996. *Keeping Life Simple*. Storey
Luhrs, J. 1997. *The Simple Living Guide*. Broadway Books
Maslow, A.H. 1999. *Toward a Psychology of Being*. Wiley, 3rd edition
Shaughnessy, S. 1993. *Walking on Alligators*. Harper
St James, E. 1995. *Inner Simplicity*. Hyperion
St James, E. 1994. *Simplify Your Life*. Hyperion
Steward, M. 1998. *Yoga*. Teach Yourself Books
Thoreau, H.D. 1993. *Walden and Other Writings*. Barnes & Noble Classics
Wallis, V. 1999. *The Which? Guide to Money*. Which? Books

Chapter 10 *Putting it all together*
Levine, K. 1996. *Keeping Life Simple*. Storey
Meynert, L. 1989. *Life Management: live better by working smarter*. Oldcastle
Thoreau, H.D. 1993. *Walden and Other Writings*. Barnes & Noble Classics
Webber, T. 1997. Strategies for surviving and thriving in organisations. *Career Development International*, **2**, 90–2

Addresses

Association of Noise Consultants
6 Trap Road, Guilden Morden,
nr Royston, Herts SG8 0JE
Tel: (01763) 852958
Fax: (01763) 853252
Email: anc@ukgateway.net
Web site: www.association-of-noise-consultants.co.uk

British Association of Counselling
1 Regent Place, Rugby, Warwickshire
CV21 2PJ
Tel: (01788) 550899
Fax: (01788) 562189
Email: bac@bac.co.uk
Web site: www.bac.co.uk

British Confederation of Psychotherapists
37 Mapesbury Road, London
NW2 4HJ
Tel: 020–8830 5713
Fax: 020–8452 3684
Email: mail@bcp.org.uk
Web site: www.bcp.org.uk

British Council of Chinese Martial Arts
c/o 110 Frensham Drive, Popular Farm,
Nuneaton, Warwickshire CV10 9QL
Tel/Fax: 024–7639 4642
Email: info@bccma.demon.co.uk
Web site: www.bccma.org.uk

British Wheel of Yoga
1 Hamilton Place, Boston Road,
Sleaford NG34 7ES
Tel: (01529) 306851
Fax: (01529) 303680
Email: office@bwy.org.uk
Web site: www.bwy.org.uk

Buddhist Society
58 Eccleston Square, London
SW1V 1PH
Tel: 020–7834 5858
Mon–Fri 2–6pm; Sat 2–5pm
Fax: 020–7976 5238
Web site: www.buddsoc.org.uk

CanDo
Hanover House, 30–32 Charlotte
Street, Manchester M1 4FD
Tel: 0161–950 3300
Contact through web site:
www.cando.ac.uk

Ethical Consumer
Unit 21, 41 Old Birley Street,
Manchester M15 5RF
Tel: 0161–226 2929
Fax: 0161–226 6277
Email: ethicon@mcr1.poptel.org.uk
Web site: www.ethicalconsumer.org

National Debtline
Birmingham Settlement, 318 Summer
Lane, Birmingham B19 3RL
Tel: (0808) 808 4000
Lines open Mon and Thurs 10am-4pm,
Tues and Wed 10am-7pm, Fri 10am-12pm

National T'ai Chi Ch'uan Association
36 Queens Road, Leytonstone,
London E11 1BB
Tel: 020–8556 6393
Email: ntcca@demon.co.uk

The Open University
PO Box 200, Milton Keynes MK7 6YZ
Tel: (01908) 653231
Email: ces-gen@open.ac.uk
Web site: www.open.ac.uk

Regester Larkin
16 Doughty Street, London WC1N 2PL
Tel: 020–7831 3839
Fax: 020–7831 3632

Royal College of Psychiatrists
17 Belgrave Square, London
SW1X 8PG
Tel: 020–7235 2351
Fax: 020–7245 1231
Web site: www.rcpsych.ac.uk

Royal National Institute for the Blind
224 Great Portland Street, London
W1N 6AA
Tel: 020–7388 1266
Fax: 020–7388 2034
Web site: www.rnib.org.uk

Royal National Institute for Deaf People
PO Box 16461, London EC1 8TT
Helpline: (0808) 808 0123
Text phone: (0808) 808 9000
Fax: 020–7296 8199
Email: helpline@rnid.org.uk
Web site: www.rnid.org.uk

SOPHIE (Secretaries of Pharmaceutical
Industry Executives)
75 Sheen Lane, East Sheen, London
SW14 8AD
Tel: 020–8878 8566
Fax: 020–8876 8834
Web site: www.sophiefriends.com

Talking Life
PO Box 1, Wirral CH47 7DD
Tel: 0151–632 0662
Fax: 0151–632 1206
Web site: www.talkinglife.co.uk

Transcendental Meditation
Freepost, London SW15 2PN
Tel: (08705) 143733
Fax: (01695) 727499
Email: tminfo@maharishi.org.uk
Web site:
www.transcendental-meditation.org.uk

Voluntary Services Overseas (VSO)
317 Putney Bridge Road, London
SW15 2PN
Tel: 020–8780 7200
Fax: 020–8780 7300
Email: enquiry@vso.org.uk
Web site: www.vso.org.uk

Which? Books
Freepost, PO Box 44, Hertford X
SG14 1YB
Tel: (0800) 252100
Fax: (0800) 533053
Web site: www.which.net

Yoga for Health Foundation
Ickwell Bury, Ickwell, Biggleswade
SG18 9EF
Tel: (01767) 627271
Fax: (01767) 627445

Internet links

Many of the time and life management sites on the World Wide Web are either subtle or blatant advertisements for products and services. These sites offer free services, although there may be some advertisements on the sites or e-zines.

- Accessibility sites: Microsoft (http://microsoft.com/enable/); Apple (http://apple.com/disability/).
- *Frozen Assets* – http://members.aol.com/OAMCLoop/index.html – offers advice on how to 'Cook for a Day and Eat for a Month'.
- *Inpharm*: www.inpharm.com
- *Simple Times* (http://members.aol.com/DSimple) is a free twice-monthly email newsletter advocating simple, frugal living. Each issue goes to around 19,000 subscribers; send a blank email message to: simple-times-subscribe@egroups.com.
- *The Frugal Life* – www.topica.com/lists/frugallife/ – has a strong US focus, but it still has some worthwhile tips.
- *The Slow Food movement* – www.slowfood.com.
- *simpleliving101* (http://www.simpleliving101.com/) – another web site with a free e-zine and numerous tips.

Index